A. Goodchild

D1808539

THE HERO
AND
THE VILLAIN

Torn Curtain Publishing
Wellington, New Zealand
www.torncurtainpublishing.com

© Copyright Jeffrey McKee, 2020
All rights reserved.

ISBN Softcover 978-0-473-50518-9
ISBN Epub 978-0-473-50519-6

The right of Jeffrey McKee to be identified as the author of this work in terms of section 96 of the Copyright Act 1994 is hereby asserted.

All rights reserved. No part of this publication may be reproduced, stored in a retrieval system, or transmitted, in any form or by any means, electronic, mechanical, photocopying, recording or otherwise, without prior permission of the copyright author.

Scripture taken from the New King James Version®. Copyright © 1982 by Thomas Nelson. Used by permission. All rights reserved.

All illustrations are taken from a series of 241 wood-engravings, designed by the French artist Gustave Doré (1832–1883) for a new deluxe edition of the 1843 French translation of the Vulgate Bible, popularly known as the Bible de Tours. This work is in the Public Domain.

A catalogue record for this book is available from the National Library of New Zealand.

To our beloved children.

Your Mum and I have spent our life gathering this and that in the spirit, boxing it up and packing it securely to pass on to you in the next generation.

I'm imagining a well-laden vehicle barrelling down the years toward you, heavy with wisdom, opportunity, privilege and blessing. We hope you climb on board to discover the biggest bundle of joy we can possibly send on before you.

You guys are true heroes in our eyes. May you find our heart and desire for you in these pages.

The Hero
and
The Villain

Jeffrey McKee

CONTENTS

HUMILITY MEETS DIVINITY 9

THE HERO AND THE VILLAIN 75

A HERO ARISES 139

INTIMACY AND AUTHORITY 205

THE HERO WITHIN 269

PART

1

HUMILITY MEETS DIVINITY

HERO WORSHIP

Who, being in very nature God,

did not consider equality with God something to be used to his own advantage;

rather, he made himself nothing

by taking the very nature of a servant,

being made in human likeness.

And being found in appearance as a man,

he humbled himself

by becoming obedient to death—

even death on a cross!

Philippians 2:6-8

Eliezer and Rebekah

CHAPTER ONE

HUMILITY INCARNATE

SUDDENLY WE WERE ACTIVELY ENGAGED
AND INVOLVED IN WELCOMING HIS
GOODNESS INTO OUR WORLD.

It makes a lot of difference which lens we bring to bear on God. While our day-to-day approach to Him does not diminish or magnify Him personally, it does have the potential to significantly change us and our trajectory in life. Our default setting when we come at God influences everything.

I remember the impact in our family when we stopped focussing on the sovereignty of God and started honing in on His goodness instead. We were used to saying things like, "God is still on the throne." It brought comfort when things were going wrong, and gave us some sense of security, but it also made us a bit passive. After all, if He had everything in hand, our actions made very little difference.

Still, an emphasis on God's sovereignty was foundational to us. It informed our faith and made us expectant of God's deliverance.

And then it happened. . .

We discovered that God was good.

He is good. We already knew this, of course, but suddenly the fact that God is good became vitally important.

It became the default lens through which we subsequently viewed God.

Ps 100:5

With His goodness now front and centre for us, our security became dependant on the constancy of His goodness rather than on His absolute power.

There is no shadow of turning in Him.

God is good . . . all the time!

He doesn't wake up on the wrong side of bed and backhand us like a pesky bug.

No, He's always good and only gives good gifts. End of story.

This lens illuminated the redemptive purposes of God for us in a stunning way. Suddenly we began to focus on Him as 'the one whose eyes move to and fro throughout the whole earth, strongly supporting those whose hearts are completely his.' God is good, and He wants only good for us. Now the bad stuff in the world made more sense. We could acknowledge it without the necessity of seeing Him as its source. Instead, we saw Him busy working *against* darkness and despair, working all things together to somehow produce good outcomes!

As we started to look at God differently, our view of ourselves gradually changed too. We began to realise that God desired for each us to become an epicentre for the release of His redemptive purposes in this world. His goodness brought goodness into our lives. We were ready to receive it, and it overflowed to bless those around us. Excitement rose, and we were caught up in the joy of what God was doing. No longer were we loyal but passive subjects of a sovereign God. Instead, we were partners with Him, actively engaged and involved in welcoming the goodness of God into our lives and into our world.

The God-is-good lens acknowledged our brokenness and bondage and showed us that God was not the author of evil, pain and hurt. It allowed us to recognise the enemy of our souls, the baggage we carried and the broken world we inhabited. It wasn't pleasant, but at least black was black and white was white. Light and darkness were not confused; God, in His persistent goodness, was always ready to transform a situation as we brought it into the light and invited Him in.

James 1:17 | **Matt 7:11** | **2 Chr 16:9** | **Rom 8:28** | **2 Cor 6:1** | **James 1:13**

With this shift, we grew up a little, lost our spiritual innocence a little, and yet the freedom, healing and perspective we gained were worth it. If maturity in scripture stems from the ability to discern good from evil, this new lens moved us forward on our journey . . . a little deeper and a little higher.

The paradigm of the goodness of God opened us up for a lot of personal healing, and slowly we began to discover how to effectively lead others into their own breakthroughs. We were no longer confused as to the author of misfortune; now we became confident and even a little eager, ready to address its existence wherever we saw it. We were content with the goodness of God. We saw no need for anything additional.

But there was more to be had.

Years later, we discovered God was humble.

God is sovereign. God is good. And now . . .

"What? God is humble?"

I know, it seems a little weird.

When I informed my twelve-year-old daughter that God is humble, she immediately told me off. She said what you are possibly saying right now.

"But what about the glory and honour? Isn't He the Most High—the Almighty?"

"Yes."

"But humility doesn't compute with divinity and glory! What do you mean?"

"Agreed. It is a challenge to contemplate the humility of God—and even more difficult to understand."

Yes, praising God is a worthy occupation. He inhabits those praises; He is attracted to praise. Praise and worship powerfully change the atmosphere and invite God-orchestrated revival into our hearts and lives. It's true that God deserves all honour.

Heb 5:15 | Ps 22:3 | Rom 16:27 | 1 Pet 4:11

But the way humility operates is suprising. It's not about what is yours by right, your worth or your position. It is about your attitude to those things, and to others. Both are possible at the same time. God is glorious. God is also humble. And once the realisation of it takes root in our hearts, there is no recovery.

Q1.   What is your go-to lens when you think of God?

Q2.   What is your response to the suggestion of God as humble?

Q3.   Describe your journey. In what ways has your perception of God changed along the way?

Prayer.

Lord. High and humble God, we want to know You better, and so we invite You to overwhelm us. Show us Your glory, Lord. Show Your heart. And help us to stoop to find You in the lowest place.   Amen.

CHAPTER TWO

MEETING OF HUMBLE HEARTS

DESPITE BROKEN DREAMS AND UNREALISED
EXPECTATIONS, SHE SAID YES, AND HER
DESTINY WAS RELEASED.

It stands to reason. When God behaves in a dignified manner, ensuring he stands somewhat aloof, He should attract more glory and honour from people.

We do our best. We talk Him up as though it does Him a favour—and yet it seems He unconscionably neglects this priority Himself. He knows what it takes us years to uncover . . . that patience and humility are the best antidote for our obsession with ourselves. He breaks our pride with a gentle touch.

God was not in the fire or the storm.

He was in the still, small voice.

He comes without pretention, then looks for the same in us. It's only when our posture matches His own and we bring full-hearted affirmation to His quietly spoken promptings that His redemptive purposes are powerfully and beautifully unleashed in our lives and our world.

He looks on the heart, and what He finds when He looks deep inside is crucial. After all, if it's to be found at all, that is where humility resides.

He wants to know if we will join Him in His humility.

Will we align ourselves by making humility the primary defining factor of our identity too?

1 Kings 19:11-13 | 1 Sam 16:7

He comes to save the world and descends to earth in human form without even booking a room at the inn.

Humility tolerates risk. It can put itself in the hands of another.

Somehow it works . . .

Will the innkeeper say "Yes," when there is no financial gain to be made?

He does.

Will Mary say, "Yes," when it comes with a stigma?

She does, too.

Mary's *yes* is so magnificent that folks throughout history have named it *the Magnificat,* and even set it to music. Her humble words of affirmation, so deeply seated in humility, were exactly what was required. Her response to the angelic message was to feel overwhelmingly privileged that one of such low estate should be offered such a sacred task.

In the incarnation, the humility of God collided with humility within a person, and in that worshipful moment, God's kingdom came to earth. 'Be it unto me,' she replied, and with that, not only were God's purposes released, but so too was her destiny.

His purposes and our destinies stand behind a locked door.

> We hold the key.

> > He leads us to the lock.

But it takes a certain state of heart to fit the key in the lock and open the door. It takes humility.

And suddenly, all through the Bible, we find one person after another; those who are led by a humble heart and respond with an enthusiastic "Yes" to God, disregarding the cost and agreeing wholeheartedly with His desires, despite their own unresolved questions, doubts and fears.

Luke 2:7 I Luke 1:46-55

My favourite example is Rebecca. In her situation, humility came, bearing her destiny, in the form of Abraham's head-servant. Unsure of himself in the moment, the ancient man worries how he will find the right woman to be the bride of Isaac, his master's son.

He asks God for help.

"I will go to that well," he says in the direction of heaven, "and ask any women that comes by if she will give me a drink. But here is the test . . . let her offer to water my camels as well."

Though she didn't know it, Rebecca's humble heart, full of readiness to serve, was perfectly positioned for her to receive her destiny. Think about it. God had in mind for her to be the grandmother of His chosen people. He wanted to gift her with a prince for a husband, but whether or not she received it came down to her treatment of a complete stranger—an old man she had never met.

She passes the test.

Then they go home to her house, the scriptures tell us, and everything is agreed, but still there remains another "yes" for her to voice. Eliezer has accomplished his mission. He is keen to return to his master. Rebecca's family, on the other hand, wish to delay her departure—to have as much time as possible with her before she leaves. With the two parties now at an impasse, they resolve to let the girl decide, and once again, Rebecca enthusiastically steps into all God has prepared for her.

Yes, she will leave all she has know and go with the man immediately!

A posture of humility is exactly what is needed to receive what God has in mind. He approaches without fanfare or force, and the strength of our "Yes" determines everything.

The woman at the well, in remarkable contrast, is stubborn—and yet, the same mechanisms of the kingdom are at work. She too, had to find it within herself to say "Yes!" to a stranger at a well.

I imagine Jesus, leaving the presence of His father that morning, carrying her destiny in His hand. And yet, when she finally encounters him, we find her so

Gen 24:5 | Gen 24:12-21 | Gen 24: 50-57 | John 4:9

preoccupied, so ready to argue with the Son of God, that she nearly misses her moment. Jesus speaks out of frustration. He intrigues us with His words.

"If you only knew! If you only knew who you share a conversation with! If you only knew the gift of God—what He had in store for you."

But she was unaware; she would scarcely have guessed that her destiny could be so rich. The day before she was on the outer, rejected and vilified in the community. Tomorrow, she would be recognised as the one who welcomed the Messiah and brought salvation to her town.

Humility comes laden with gifts, yet this woman finds it so terribly difficult to receive from the one who holds her future. He is from another culture. He is hot and thirsty . . . dependant on her. She, however, is so combative that she even forgets His simple request for a drink. She finds it almost impossible to be agreeable.

Though the context of the release of their destinies is nearly identical—an encounter with a stranger at a well—this woman is the opposite of Rebecca in nearly every way. But eventually, her demeanour shifts. Jesus gently humbles her. Finally she is able to receive from him, and in an instant, her life is changed.

Let's come to one last scenario where Jacob is blessing Joseph, his son.

"You are a vine, my son. The vine grew over the wall."

In other words, "You were surrounded by things that could have hemmed you in, but it was not enough to hold you back! You son, have prevailed over it all!"

What was the key that allowed Joseph to lay hold of a tremendous destiny despite betrayal, slavery, imprisonment and even despair? Yes, it was humility. In Potiphar's house and later on in prison, Joseph rose above the mental anguish and pain of his terrible losses, and faithfully served.

Joseph was humility personified, and it made him ready to receive from his God, who also walks in humility. It feels strange to think of God meeting us in a humble exchange. This is not easy. This requires care. Let's take off our shoes. We are on holy ground. . .

John 4:10 | John 4:16-42 | Gen 49:22-26 | Gen 39 | Ex 3:5 | Josh 5:15

Q1.   What do you remember as the lowest time in your life? How did you deal with it and what came next for you?

Q2.   'If only you knew the gift of God.' Who has God entrusted to deliver your destiny to you? What do you believe your destiny to be?

Q3.   How can you respond with an enthusiastic "Yes" to God's humble word to you, in the context of your life right now?

Prayer.

Lord. Our dear Father, We come before You with open ears and hearts laid bare. We listen for Your word. Here we are. Speak the word. Grace us with the passion to receive what You say, and forgive the many ways we have missed Your whisper and ignored Your counsel.   Amen.

CHAPTER THREE

NO COMPROMISE

IF EVERYONE REALISED THAT GOD IS NOT
OPPRESSIVE, THE KINGDOM OF DARKNESS
WOULD GO OUT OF BUSINESS THE VERY NEXT
DAY.

Strangely enough, the humility of God doesn't actually rob Him of honour and worship. It attracts it. Let's take the example of the woman with the alabaster box of perfume—a year's wages, apparently wasted as she breaks it at the feet of Jesus. Hers was adoration in the extreme, dignified and accepted by the Lord.

Simon and his lot didn't know what to make of one who did not hold Himself above the common people. The Pharisees didn't understand humility, or the power it released to transform lives. Jesus, on the other hand, didn't guard His reputation. He didn't hold the riff-raff at arm's length; He came humbly, and consequently this woman was noticed and released from her pain.

Then, she became an exemplary worshipper.

Christ saw her heart. He saw beyond the bad choices, the poor background and the desperate struggle to survive in a harsh world. He didn't keep His distance. He stooped and came near, to know her name, to see and understand her need, and to heal.

God comes to us the same way. What does He see? What does He say to you and me?

"You are not orphans or slaves."

Matt 26:6-13 | Mark 14:3-9 | Luke 7:36-50 | John 12:1-8 | Matt 9:11 | Gal 4:6-7
John 14:18

"You are My sons and daughters."

His kind treatment of us comes as a shock. We expect God to be severe or overbearing. Sure, He wants us to be humble, but isn't that simply so that He ensures His rightful place over us?

But, no. In fact, we find ourselves discovering that He is entirely the opposite. We hear His voice . . .

"You are not a number to me. I know you by name."

"You are not a resource in My kingdom. I have called you friends."

"I don't want you as servants or slaves. You are not cannon fodder in the fulfilment of the Great Commission."

"I am your Father. You are My child. Welcome to the family."

He is not oppressive.

He never has been and never will be.

If everyone in the world realised that God is not oppressive, the kingdom of darkness would go out of business the very next day. Instead, we have listened to a pervasive lie—a lie intended to sully the character of the one who has no fault or flaw in His person.

For Him, the end never justifies the means!

In Him is light and no darkness at all—no pride, no hardness, no tyranny, no cruelty and no domination.

It begs the question, *"How does He get anything done?"*

Generally speaking, humility isn't very efficient. Consider the scale of His responsibilities. You can imagine the need for a little pragmatism, yet . . .

No darkness at all.

No pride, no hardness, no tyranny, no cruelty and no domination.

Then *how?* How do you run a kingdom on these terms?

John 1:12 | Rom 8:14-16 | 1 John 1:5

I have reflected on this at length, and the best illustration I know to describe how the humble King of heaven operates, is this parable Jesus told . . .

A king decided to hold a banquet, and so he sent out invitations. One after the other, the replies came in.

"So sorry, we cannot come!"

"Too busy at work. It's not a good time. I cannot come."

"My investments need attention. I cannot come."

"I'm getting married. I cannot come."

The king's response is pivotal.

"My banquet must be—will be filled."

But how? Will he insist—or resort to using force?

No. In the face of refusal, he remains resolute, but takes a gentle approach.

He tells his servants to go out the back alleys and find *anyone*. They don't need to be like the nobility on his original guest list.

"Go! Invite those who are hungry and sleeping rough! Compel anyone you find to come in. My banquet must be—*will be*—filled."

He doesn't send out the brute squad in response to rude refusals. There are no threats, no violence. Even though his position would permit it, he uses no force at all.

His humility is oddly combined with gritty determination.

"My banquet will be, *must be*, filled."

God is that king, and His humility means He uses invitation rather than coercion. When people are uncooperative or unresponsive, He merely extends the invitation wider.

Humility. Patience. Dogged determination.

Luke 14:15-24 | Matt 22:1-14 (a parallel where the king takes a more forceful line)

He doesn't compromise or surrender the end or the means. He will get it done, and it will be done in line with His character.

So many leaders throughout history rose with high ideals and promises to their followers, only to leave them disappointed. Maybe their leader, full of integrity and worth was rendered impotent, unable to make their mark against inertia and opposition?

Or, perhaps the one they hoped would bring such relief quickly cast aside any semblance of rectitude as their desire for influence and effectiveness eclipsed their moral compass. How many accomplishments have come at untold cost, ordinary people suffering the oppression that followed in the wake of a brutal leader?

Rarely, as we look back through time, is it possible to catch a glimpse of true greatness in leadership—and even then, the flaws are there for all to see.

Imagine if relentless determination and purpose in a leader were blended with a heart full of honour, humility and devotion to their people?

That ideal is epitomised in God Himself.

He speaks a word to express His will, and all of heaven rises to fulfil His purposes. It will eventually and inevitably come to pass. His word never returns void. Never!

His humility will not require Him to compromise His purpose, and His determination for an outcome will not cause Him to concede when it comes to His approach.

In determination *and* humility, He searches; relentlessly He seeks out the humble in heart, those who are ready with a "Yes" on their lips. He whispers a personal and immutable word quietly in their ear.

They stoop to hear and return their own word of affirmation. And heavenly vaults, packed full of priceless destiny, swing wide and burst open. Lives are flooded with all God intended for them.

He gets His way, a season of singing comes, and the beauty of the kind intention of God's heart is released.

Isa 55:11 | Song 2:10-13

Q1.   What would you say are your greatest distractions?

Q2.   How have you experienced the determination of God?

Q3.   What do you feel about the words "the end does not justify the means," both in terms of your actions toward others and theirs towards you?

Prayer.

Lord, so pure and holy. We stand in awe at the wonder of Your character—no darkness, no hardness, no tyranny, no cruelty or domination. We realise we have often failed to understand Your ways. We have dismissed Your word too soon, as if our wisdom was superior to Your own. May Your humility come to us as the antidote to our pride. Reshape us into those who love Your ways, Your precepts and Your quietly spoken word. Amen.

CHAPTER FOUR

FEAST IN ZION

BLESSING RIPPLES OUTWARDS FROM
THE GLORIOUS CAPITAL, AN ANGELIC
ENGINE HUMMING WITH LIVELY
CADENCE.

Within Jerusalem, the natural and the unseen collided. Behind the solidness of the city walls and the tactile grip of its sights and sounds, was a heavenly reality we call Zion.

The festivals in Jewish custom served to strengthen the connection, opening a window into the culture and life of heaven itself. Normal life was put on hold. Provisions were packed and loaded. Haste in the air prevented late arrival. Throughout the land, thousands of families set off with a shared intent.

It was time to go up to Jerusalem for the feast.

As we look back on those days and watch the faithful gather, a deeper reality flits across our consciousness. With eyes of the heart, we find ourselves observing a similar assembly, in the heavenlies, in distant ages past. Myriads of swarming winged creatures—angelic beings—eagerly turn from their wide-ranging responsibilities across the cosmos. Joy and anticipation fill the air, for Zion's feast is the zenith of their calendar. All around, we hear spontaneous exclamations as friends reunite.

And finally, they all take their place at an enormous table. They sit. They feast. They celebrate. They dance. They sing.

2 Sam 5:7 | 1 Kings 8:1 | Ps 2:6 | Ps 14:7 | Luke 2:41 | Ps 120-134 | Isa 33:20

It is a time of honouring exploits and worshipping their Lord. It is a moment for laughter, joy and ease for those whose unceasing labour administers the pervasive kingdom of God. Then, the feast concludes.

Heavenly life resumes.

Time passes.

Until . . . a little later, the peace and rhythm of heaven is disrupted.

Treason! A bitter rift ensues. War rages on too long. The toll of the conflict becomes unspeakable. Then, at last, the tide is turned. Satan and the angels who had rallied to him against the Lord are finally cast out. They are cast down.

And as the clamour of conflict ceased, the reverberations of energetic restoration activities are heard. Heavenly life resumes. Once more, the kingdom stretches to its full height, and blessing again ripples outwards from its glorious capital, an angelic engine humming with lively cadence.

On and on, they labour, without restraint or hesitation. If there were days, weeks, months or years in heaven we would say they swept by without any fundamental change.

Until something entirely different happens.

Suddenly, an array of bells peal jubilantly from a tower high on the glorious city's walls, their generous music echoing throughout the land and into realms beyond.

Angels everywhere turn their faces toward its source. They stop everything they are doing. There is a pause fit to startle a casual observer.

Work ceases in paradise.

The time of feast and festival has returned once more, and with it comes a sense of relief, for this is a tangible sign that heaven has returned to normal. And yet, there is also pain; after the war, many old friends and comrades will not be part of this celebration.

Ezek 28 | Rev 12 | Jude 1:6 | Isa 14:12

The loyal and devoted flood the streets of Zion. The celestial capital is awash with delight. Here and there the marks of battle remain discernible, yet all is forgotten as heaven takes stock of those who remain. Some search in vain to find faces in the crowd only to realise they have fallen, never to have a place at the great feast again.

The Lord surveys the gathered throng, thoroughly joyful. He takes in each face, and responds with recognition and pleasure. Then, He steps aside and momentarily gazes at an entire section of the table, full of empty seats. First we see sorrow, and then other emotions take their turn on His face, each fleeting across His expression. Finally, a determined glint appears in His eyes, just as He ascends the dais to speak.

"Welcome into My joy. The feast, with all its scents and colour is upon us. It delights My heart to see you all here together. Yes, it is true. Darkness has touched our land, yet we have prevailed at last. Your victories are many. They have been written in the books. Your tireless efforts to defend and restore our realm have been noticed. The court scribes have left no detail out. Later, they will be opened and read. At this feast, more than any prior, there are so many honours to bestow. But, first things first. They tell Me all things are now ready . . ."

Cheers erupt, and we can only imagine the splendour of the banquet as it is served. We hear the hum of innumerable voices speaking over one another, the clink of utensils on plates and the tinkle of glasses raised together in mutual acknowledgement as tales of the intervening season are recounted.

The festive tradition salves wounds and restores hope. It relieves the tension formed by the exertions of the season just passed. A lightness returns to the kingdom. Even the Lord as He walks from table to table is caught up in the moment. Yet watching closely, we see Him circle around to stand behind an empty place. He walks along a silent row of perfectly positioned chairs, and His hands brush their translucent fabric as He is caught in a reverie.

A hush descends on the hall; voices quiet as others notice their king's pain. A mighty angel observes the change and quickly rises to attend his lord, leading

Luke 14:17 | Rev 5:11

Him back into the crowd and into the moment. Joy returns to the great hall, but in a way, we—and they—have inadvertently beheld the heart of God.

It is well into the feast when our Lord rises to speak once again. He opens His mouth and releases an immutable word.

"There will come a time when My table will be full once more."

Hundreds of thousands of chairs scrape in a loud rumble as every guest is roused to stand in unison. Clapping and cheering, they cry out at the display of divine resolve. The joyous and carefree atmosphere of the feast has changed to one of awe and worship as they feel the weight of this word and realise, this will be an absolute mission to accomplish!

In His humility, God did not force rebel angels to worship and obey him. Evil angels were dispossessed because they cared more for each other, profit and opportunity than they cared about the Lord and their privileged place at His table. In response, He would not force their will to bend to his. Instead, He would see to it that every empty place was freshly occupied. When they returned to their work, He and the host of heaven would begin a determined effort to fulfil this ultimate prerogative.

And that has shaped all of history.

In response, creation birthed humankind. As one generation followed the next, the unrelenting word of God conveyed a quiet invitation to privileged individuals down through the ages:

"Come, take your place at My feast."

Throughout all of time, angels have ranged wide and far, bearing the invitation, compelling whoever would listen, to take the place of the fallen. And all the while, humble determination sits upon the throne of heaven watching and waiting for His word to eventually come to pass.

When the first faithful heart accepted the invitation, bringing with his sacrifice to God an appreciation of things beyond this world,dispossessed angels stricken with dark jealousy, rose up to take revenge and oppose God's new

Ezek 28:5

plan and purpose. Shortly afterward Abel lay dead and cold, killed by the hand of his brother, and yes, there was grief in his family. The first murder on earth was a dark day indeed. And yet, something had shifted.

The first empty seat had been filled in the banquet hall of heaven.

One down, many more left to go.

Gen 4:1-15 | Heb 11:4

Q1.   Why is it so difficult to acknowledge the problems and disfunction in heaven's past, given the almost universal belief it took place?

Q2.   What is your response to the offer of a place at the table?

Q3.   How would you expect God to respond to personal loss, pain and regrettable circumstances in His life?

Prayer.

Lord. We stand with You in Your passion to redeem what has been broken and restore what has been lost. We want to take our place at Your banquet table, and we desire to be part of the band around You, determined to set things right. Help us to contribute to Your cause in this world, so we can live a lifestyle that restores joy to Your heart, when so much has conspired to operate outside of Your will and ways. Make us holy and make us good—ransomed, healed, restored and forgiven. Make us a force for good in this world, ready to carry Your great invitation.   Amen.

CHAPTER FIVE

ENTERING IN

PETER DROPPED IN FOR LUNCH AT A
CENTURION'S HOUSE. THE MISSION BECAME
GLOBAL AND THE INVITATION WENT VIRAL.

Abel was at the beginning, but the mission continued to progress with each successive generation. And while the Bible is many things, in its essence it simply retells the utter difficulty of what the Lord and His angels had set out to achieve.

Who would respond to a mystical invitation to dine at an unseen table?

Within the list of *begets* and *begats* in the early pages of the Bible, it is a challenge to decipher who actually made the grade. We are left to wonder who among them had sufficient faith to take hold of an inheritance beyond the tactile and tangible.

Enoch is an easy pick. I love his audacity. He lived so many centuries before Christ, the cross and the torn veil—long before official access was given into the heavenlies through the death of Christ. And yet, he so embraced heaven's reality, that he was literally awash with the Father's presence and the life of God until, in effect, he belonged much more *there* than *here*. Enoch didn't die and then go to heaven. He had already made himself comfortable *there*; he simply lingered in the joy of God and then one day simply disappeared from earth's point of view.

The number of seats being filled, gradually climbed higher.

Time went by.

Eventually, the humble determination of God focussed on a single man—Abraham, who rose to become a nation. Not only did Abraham's faith assure him of a seat at the table; in God's heart was a great desire that Abraham's offspring would make up the places at the feast still uninhabited. "Look toward the heavens, and count the stars, if you are able to count them," says God, as His heart beats with anticipation. "So shall your descendants be," a nation birthed for one specific purpose—to repopulate His banquet table.

God went to great lengths to make it as easy as possible for his descendants, the children of Israel. He created a copy of Zion in Jerusalem, their capital. He gave them replicas of the heavenly feasts, and filled their culture with shadows of things from above. He even came in Shekinah glory to inhabit their place of worship. Everywhere they looked, they were being invited up into the reality behind the imagery. Heaven was right in front of their faces.

But human hearts are easily distracted and often dull to what is beyond this world. And, the kingdom of darkness was always ready to draw attention away.

It would always be a fight for one to take their place at the heavenly table.

Some rose and answered the invitation. Many did not.

After centuries of patience the invitation began to clarify. The incarnation of our Lord, His all-sufficient sacrifice, the torn curtain, and the dispensation of the Holy Spirit all favoured the mission of God to fill His banquet table. The essence of the mission remained unchanged, yet the Jewish people become increasingly unresponsive to the invitation.

And so, true to His nature, our humble and determined God simply opened the door wider.

Peter dropped in for lunch at a centurion's house, and the Holy Spirit fell on all his family.

That day would become a watershed moment.

Gen 12:1-3 | Gen 15:5 | Col 2:16-17 | 2 Chron 7:1-3 | Acts 2 | Acts 10

Everything changed. The mission had become global, and the invitation went viral.

At another significant moment along the way, a man staggers at the news he has just heard. The might of Rome has turned against his nation. Thousands of Jews have been slaughtered. Jerusalem has been devastated and the temple is destroyed.

With his first thought being for his brothers and sisters scattered throughout the empire, this anonymous man takes up a quill and writes an open letter to them all. The date is AD70, and we call his letter, the book of Hebrews.

He wants to articulate the mission of God down through history. He wants them to hear the invitation once again! All that has gone before is just a prelude to what comes to us in Christ. The temple and all its sacrifices and imagery in Jerusalem were now gone, but not to worry! He urges his readers to seize the moment and embrace the spiritual substance and reality that all the physical structures and ceremony made with human hands had portrayed in shadow.

He recounts a list of those of whom the world was not worthy—the greats of old. By faith they saw that there was more at stake, he explains. They looked for a different city—the real thing! The invitation had come to them and with it a desire for their place in the city on high. It was in their heart to answer the call to come and feast in Zion, the city of the great king.

The author describes a great crowd of witnesses, those who have taken their place at the table, and now cheer us on as we receive a similar opportunity and invitation.

His clarion call is for each of his readers to enter in, to follow Jesus in through the veil, and into the joy of God.

And so we rise and step forward. We lift a hand and draw aside the heavy torn cloth. Our physical awareness recedes, and as we heed the nameless writer we find ourselves lifted into a beautiful and glorious pandemonium — a kaleidoscope of sights and sounds set to completely overwhelm our spiritual senses.

Heb 9:24 l Col 2:17 l Heb 11 l Ps 48:2 l Heb 10:19-23 l Heb 3:7-4:11

"What's happening? Where are we?!"

Our unidentified guide is just as captivated by the moment as we are.

He answers, "We have come to Mount Zion, to the city of the living God, the heavenly Jerusalem. You have come to thousands upon thousands of angels in joyful assembly. Enter into the joy of the Lord. Take your places at the table. Welcome to the feast!"

Heb 12:18-24 | Matt 25:21-23 | Luke 22:29

Q1.   How are you heeding God's invitation to enter in?

Q2.   Who in the list of the great cloud of witnesses do you identify with most?

Q3.   When you consider your relationship to the purposes of God, how could that guide your think about your destiny and purpose?

Prayer.

Lord, You are the real thing and Your abode defines reality and truth. We live among the shadows. We worship You for truth, more substantive that anything we can ask, think or imagine. We repent, for we realise our poor hearts find too much comfort in the concrete and mundane. Your ways are higher than ours, so we ask You to lead us in ways everlasting, unto Yourself and into life in all its fullness. We answer Your call. We take our place in Christ, seated with Him in heavenly places.   Amen.

CHAPTER SIX

DECONSTRUCTION

WE NEED TO CONSIDER DISPOSSESSION
AS AN INEVITABLE OUTCOME OF GOD'S
REDEMPTIVE PURPOSE AND APPROACH.

I don't know if you have ever taken something apart and laid out all the pieces. Okay, it's true, the thing might never actually function again. And yet, as we dismantle it, we get to figure out how it ticks, how it works, how it runs.

Right now, let's take apart the way God works, like we took the toaster or the remote control car apart when we were twelve years old.

Out comes a screwdriver, and if we hold our tongue just right, we may be able to prise it all apart and convince this mysterious object to render up its secrets.

Here's the first piece: Humility.

God is humble, but humility in isolation is feeble, right?

It's true. He is more complicated than that. We'll need to go further and dig out more if we are ever to figure Him out.

We look again . . .

Next comes determination. We lay it out on the cloth upon the table as well.

Let's press the two together. Feel the hum of their combined power? Nothing on earth can match the potential of humility paired with determination.

Patience comes out next, also seemingly an essential part. We mess with it a bit and try coupling and decoupling it with humility and determination to test their fit and connection.

Finally we lay them down, side by side on the table.

Next, we extract . . . invitation.

The parts are no longer in situ, but our curiosity drives us to tinker. We're attempting to connect them, to get them to work together outside of where they were found in the heart and mind of God.

Could they work in our lives too?

Before our very eyes we have a demonstration of the way God works and thinks, one that is utterly intriguing.

Not satisfied, however, we unscrew and withdraw more componentry. We attach buttons back onto the functional model. There they are,

　　　Rejection and . . . acceptance!

As we screw them into place, we find these have consequences. One is wired into life and blessing and the other is connected to ruin. Now we can trigger and interact with the display.

A final piece is extracted and added into the vibrant simulation. What shall we call this? Eventually we identify it as dispossession.

We stand back to reflect on our work, watching the cogs and dials as they interact together. All of life is here. This is how God operates. It gives us a sense of cause and effect, of wisdom in its purest form.

As we observe, we begin to contemplate.

Dispossession seems a particularly harsh component. Could it really be an inevitable part of the workings of heaven? The answer is, yes.

When I took a look at how dispossession pervades the scriptures, it was nearly unbelievable. It is everywhere!

Evil angels were dispossessed; others will ultimately take their place at the feast. So were the Canaanites—Israel took their place in the Promised Land after their iniquity reached a full measure. David dispossessed Saul. Jacob took the place of his brother, Esau.

The closer we look, the more we realise we're onto something! Look at Vashti and Esther, Absalom and Solomon, Haman and Mordechai, Judas and Matthias, Moses and Joshua. In every one of these cases, we find dispossession at play. Dispossession is clearly a necessary and important component in the way God deals with people.

If we wish to understand our God, the world we live in, and the causes and consequences that determine how our own lives play out, we need to factor in this vital element of dispossession.

Now the model on the table is more than a delightful blur of motion and action.

As we have examined the inner workings of the heart of God, we have discovered a dynamic that both explains our relationship with God *and* empowers our everyday life.

Jude 1:6 | Gen 15:16 | Ex 23:23-33 | 2 Sam 5:1-5 | Gen 27 | Est 2:17 | 2 Sam 18-1 Kings 1 Esther 8:2 | Acts 1:15-26 | Josh 1:1

Q1.   What is your go-to approach to tackling difficult problems in your life?

Q2.   How does your approach to a challenge compare to God's—a combination of humility, determination, patience, and invitation?

Q3.   How has your perception of God and His ways developed over time?

Prayer.

Lord, we reflect on a lifetime of missed opportunities and reasons You should justifiably cast us aside and move on to others, and yet we find reason to hope in Your unfailing love. Tarry a little longer with us. Keep us as the apple of Your eye. We want to do better, to walk nearer, to see more clearly through the lens of humility. We desire to be strengthened in patience and perseverance to see Your redemptive purposes realised in our lives and our times.   Amen.

CHAPTER SEVEN

WRESTLING

**EVERY BUMP AND BRUISE WE SUFFER IS HOLY
AND PRECIOUS, AND WE SHOULD COUNT THEM
ALL WITH A JOY-FILLED HEART.**

Now that we've looked at how God 'ticks,' we need to ask what it all means for us as we live in the physical world? I mean, if you are like me, that is what you need. Something that makes a difference day to day.

Funnily enough, I find myself thinking about Jacob.

He's just packed up his entire household and now they're on their way to their new home. It's been a big few days. It takes a decent amount of effort to relocate a family the size of Jacob's.

Truth be told, Jacob is afraid of what lies ahead. He's taking steps, but he's full of hesitation. And so Jacob pauses to take a breath. Night is falling, the family are settling down for some much-needed rest, and the next thing Jacob knows is . . . he's being attacked! Some guy has emerged out of nowhere, and suddenly they're locked in a mortal struggle.

It turns out he was being pummelled by Jehovah God.

What?! Why is God beating up on Jacob? If Jacob really carries the promises and blessing of his grandfather Abraham, why on earth would YHWH set Himself against him? If ever we need to figure out what makes God tick, it's now. What was God thinking?!

Hos 12:4 | Gen 32:22-32

All night they wrestle, Jacob and God, until the first hint of dawn appears in the sky—and it's then that we realise that something has changed. Jacob is not the same man he was last night. He's limping, for a start, but there's more to it than that. Something has intrinsically shifted during the course of the fight. Jacob's destiny has been released, and now it is imperative for him to be renamed. From that point on, Jacob would be known as *Israel*.

And yet, we have not answered the question. What was really in play that night? Why, right when we would expect God to be on Jacob's side, did He become his adversary?

Joshua encountered a similar anomaly. As he surveyed the huge walls of Jericho and considered the monumental task of bringing them down, a great and awesome warrior appeared. The man was built like a tank but had the bearing of a prince. Having never seen Him before, Joshua asks the obvious question, "Whose side are you on?"

The answer provided by the mysterious stranger is as unnerving now as it must have been then. "Neither. But as commander of the armies of God, I come."

Really?! YHWH, Lord of the Angel Armies is impartial? At a time like this?! Joshua was about to lead the people of God into the Promised Land! Was God suddenly washing His hands of any responsibility for the outcome? Surely it was God's problem to get this job done. How else would His people be expected to fight the giants and take the territory as their own?

What do we make of the fact that both Jacob and Joshua encountered the Lord, both were positioned to receive a God-promised, physical inheritance, and yet the Lord seems to be either against them, or, at best, ambivalent. *Why?*

We need to look again at the God-components we carefully laid out.

Humility, determination, patience, invitation . . . and dispossession.

Somewhere among those factors there must be an explanation for this seemingly strange behaviour of God.

Gen 32:28 | Gen 32:32 | Josh 5:13-15

It's clear that in both cases, dispossession is a pivotal concept. Both Jacob and Joshua encountered an unexpected facet of YHWH during a milestone moment in the dispossession of the Canaanites from the Promised Land. But that still doesn't explain why YHWH gave Jacob and Joshua trouble. Dispossession should mean that *it's time!* If God's people are about to advance, God should be on their side, right?

As it happens, even on a triumphant day of dispossession, God's heart is as much for the ones whose place and position is about to be lost, as for those who will undoubtedly take their place, and so He comes to Jacob and to Joshua, not as a friend looking for communion, but as the one who arbitrates righteousness and justice on the earth.

He is here, as leader of the host of heaven, to ensure that the dispossession transaction is right and just.

God's promise is sure, His word immutable, His gifts and calling irrevocable, His character consistent and His gifts always good. And yet, on these occasions His thoughts and actions turn on a knife edge.

They could go either way.

The moment of dispossession has arrived.

Everything is ready for a transaction in the spirit. One will gain much at the expense of the other.

One party has positioned themselves for blessing. They are about to receive an inheritance.

The other has crossed a line. It is all over for them now.

Jehovah draws near to oversee the matter as an objective arbitrator; with no one to represent Canaan, YHWH spars on their behalf. He comes against Jacob incarnated as a perfectly matched rival as He wrestles for the party that is being dispossessed.

And so we catch a glimpse of two men rolling around by the river, each struggling to gain the advantage. They beat each other fiercely with desperate

Josh 5:14 | Isa 55:11 | Rom 11:29 | James 1 | Gen 32

blows, each trying to obtain the upper hand, but neither can prevail. This is a fair fight, one that goes on and on through the hours of darkness.

Dawn soon came, however, and unbeknown to Jacob it marked a moment when the blessing would pass to him and his descendants. At dawn, his dynasty would be enriched—at the expense of the Canaanites, the current people of the land.

What happens just before dawn sheds a light on the heart of God even for these poor idolaters, *for the ones who are about to be dispossessed.*

We love His graciousness and enjoy His mercy and kindness, often generously bestowed in the direction of the people of God. What is more difficult for us to cope with, is His *unexpected* behaviour. How is it that we can be doing His will and laying hold of His promises, only to find that everything has such a propensity to fall apart, and so suddenly?

What is with the desperate below-the-belt swipe as God attempts to thwart Jacob's victory and prevent the Canaanite's defeat at the eleventh hour? It's a good thing Jacob held on. Despite the pain and limitation, his determination rose to a crescendo. No way was he giving up now. Jacob would have his blessing!

He wins.

And we say, "Well, good thing too! He was *meant* to win. He carried the promises!"

So Jacob comes away with a new name and a new future, and yet he limps for the rest of his life simply because YHWH couldn't stand the fact that an entire people group would soon be dispossessed, that the Canaanites would finally fall from grace. It got to him—and in a show of holy overwhelm, the Lord injures someone close to his heart, in a futile attempt to extend more grace to those who have only ever shunned it.

We didn't expect that of God.

That was a bridge too far, right?

Gen 32:25-26

In a similar scenario, when the sin of the Amorites had reached its full measure, Joshua and the Israelites entered their territory to take it. This time the wrestle lasted seven days. Joshua was fighting with the same objective as Jacob—he wanted to take the land as an inheritance for his own people.

With great faith, the people of God march around and around Jericho, their show of determination, passion and resolve finally securing their victory.

But again, God is not comfortable with this moment of dispossession. It seems, there is always a thought in His mind that patience might win them back, that a slightly longer wait or a more generous dispensation of grace might save them from the consequences of their actions.

The unseen structure and forces that govern cause and effects on earth are a clear and predictable reflection of His character, but they are also loose enough to accommodate His interventions—His grace and undeserved mercy.

Today, we stand somewhere in that space with him, thankful that the very qualities in God that challenge us most, are in fact, responsible for the reality that we are alive and standing blameless before him.

We know God wants to bless His people. He has not only granted us every spiritual blessing in the heavenlies, but His desire is for us to enjoy physical blessings on earth as well. Yet both of these can be hindered in a myriad of ways. The world, the flesh and the devil to try to hold us back, as we would expect. Our own brokenness and woundedness work against us too. That all makes sense.

But this wrestling with God in order to receive our inheritance? This is a new idea entirely. Regardless of the promises we have received, and even in spite of the sense that the timing is right, God Himself may send our expectations into a spin. He could pummel us. He might even fight a little dirty, as we close in on our objective.

But before we get irked with the Almighty and cry foul, take a moment to consider the wonder of what is taking place. Every bump and bruise we suffer is holy and precious, and we should count them all with a joy-filled heart, as with

Gen 15:16 | Josh 6:15 | Eph 1:3-4 | 3 John 1:2 | Matt 13:1-23 | James 1:2-4

every blow, God bares His soul and works into us a future filled with blessing.

It seems to hurt Him more than it hurts us.

What posture should we adopt for such a moment?

While a worshipful and quiet moment on our knees seems appropriate, most likely we find ourselves straining and sweating, grunting and groaning while the dear Lord works off His angst at what is going down. Probably best, then, to worship the matchless character of God with a determined glint in our eye and hold on tight until the break of day!

Q1.   Which do you struggle with more, God's gift to you of an inheritance at the detriment of another, or another prospering at your expense?

Q2.   When did you receive an unfair advantage? Who lost out so you could enjoy good fortune?

Q3.   When did you wrestle with God and what came out of this encounter for you?

Prayer.

Lord. You love the wayward, the broken and the rebel and though they have long spurned and forsaken You. We see they have no more devoted champion than yourself. We are stirred to emulate Your truly selfless heart, to bear a blow or two as we wrestle to turn back the negative consequences in the lives of the dispossessed. We find ourselves spoiling for a different kind of fight and asking to be welcomed in to join You in that.   Amen.

CHAPTER EIGHT

MISDIRECTION

THE CROWD QUICKLY BECAME PUPPETS IN THE HANDS OF THE ONE WHO REVELS IN VIOLENCE AND DEATH.

As I read about the crusades, it was the interplay between the natural and spiritual that struck me. No doubt, good and evil were intertwined in the motivations and actions of all involved as a strong sense of draw towards Jerusalem, turned into an apparently holy force, driving the mass of Christendom towards its own regrettable version of jihad.

What an affront to the Gospel.

It was a bloody stain on their cross-embossed surcoats.

Of course, hindsight is wonderful. We look back and shake our head in disbelief. How could anyone think this should be done in Jesus' name?

It's easy to hold tainted history at arm's length.

What were they thinking? Unbelievable!

There is good. There is bad. *This was bad.*

I agree. It was inherently evil. Still, I believe there was a misdirected seed of goodness deep in their hearts.

I first learned about the kingdom of darkness' mastery in the art of misdirection in the presence of the Lord. It was a concept I had never grasped before. The context was an ongoing and constant struggle with sin in my life. In this case, prayer didn't seem to work. More effort was no antidote. I had almost given up.

Then the Lord came to me . . .

"I want you to understand what happens when you sin."

"Okay, sure," I answered. "Some perspective would be gold."

I was tired of it all, but I listened to what He said . . .

"This is what happens."

"Yes?"

"I draw near to you, Jeff, closer and closer, and as I come close, your spirit and body respond to My proximity."

"What you say makes sense."

"You feel stirred up because I am near—it's a hunger or a thirst for me, something which only communion with Me can truly satisfy. But the Evil One sees what is happening and he hurries to arrive first. He determines to divert you. He whispers in your ear; he interprets the desire you feel to you as a need for something else, something other than me—in fact, *anything* other than me!"

As I processed His words over the following week, I mourned the opportunities for encounter with God I had missed over a lifetime of sin and temptation.

And then I became furious, because I realised . . .

I had been set up to fail.

Every time.

When I was tempted, it didn't matter whether I had given in, or stood my ground and resisted to the point of exhaustion. Either way, I had missed the opportunity to hang out with God, and that made me grumpy.

It meant, no matter what I did, I never won!

"Bring on the next round," I decided. I couldn't wait for temptation to strike. For the first time in my life, I had the sort of perspective I needed.

Weeks passed. Maybe the Devil was onto the fact that I was finally onto him. In any case, eventually, he couldn't resist—yet I could! I felt God's presence in the room and this time, I recognised it for what it was.

Rather than steeling myself for another water-boarding session like a man incarcerated by the enemy, I spoke up and told Satan where to go. Then, I welcomed the Lord in, and had the most profound and delightful time, hosting His presence.

It turns out that the Devil doesn't need to devise a huge temptation in order to us to fall. He just needs to take something good, then corrupt it slightly, or rename it or simply point us in the wrong direction.

He loves to confuse the natural and the spiritual, the good and the evil, and without a moment's hesitation, like veritable lemmings, we head for the cliff's edge.

We are easy prey.

Let's come back to the crusades . . .

I see men in armour, fighting to gain Jerusalem—a physical copy of a heavenly city called Zion, their quest turns out to be a minor misdirection with major consequences. Instead of being drawn to the presence of God and taking their place at the heavenly feast, the crusaders marched toward an earthly city, created a bloodbath, and became puppets in the hands of the one who revels in violence and death—the Devil himself. Christianity has had a global brand problem ever since.

And for us, the temptation is always to do the things we don't want to do, to fight against flesh and blood, to grow weary in well-doing, to store up treasure on earth, to love the world, and to set our minds on things below.

We've become a sorry mess. And then,

> when it feels like we can't go on,

> > and we are hemmed in by consequences of our own making,

> > > and hope is fading fast . . .

Rom 7:15 | Eph 6:12 | Gal 6:9 | Matt 6:19-21 | 1 John 2:15 | Col 3:2

When the enemy has played us for a fool one too many times, and the world has lost its glint and glory in our eyes, His messengers whisper our name, and bring an invitation that causes our hearts to leap.

"There's food and enough to spare, in my Father's house!"

Finally we turn for home.

Luke 15:17-20

Q1.   When has the enemy misdirected you, causing you to completely lose out on something the Lord wanted for you?

Q2.   What physical thing does the enemy use most to distract you? What heavenly reality is your birth-right instead?

Q3.   If you knew God wanted to spend time with you, how would you respond? What would you do?

Prayer.

Lord. We stand in truth and light and speak out against the liar and the thief, who steals our joy and all You have for us. We refuse to be manipulated by evil, and we stand for those we love as well. We choose Your presence, Your wonder and Your love. We push into the invitation of Your heavenly courts and seek Your face once more, knowing that Your heart and hands are extended toward us again.   Amen.

CHAPTER NINE

CHOOSING YOUR BATTLES

FOR A SECOND THE LORD HAD BARED
HIS SOUL TO ME, AND I GLIMPSED
SOMETHING UNFORGETTABLE.

It was a personal and very sacred encounter. The setting was a conservative Islamic city nestled at the foot of a great mountain, and every Christian in town knew what we meant when we referred to a dark cloud hanging over the city.

It was always there, quietly menacing.

It was the most remarkable thing. You could get on an intercity bus, and about an hour out of town you would find yourself suddenly happy. Why? For a simple reason. You weren't under the spiritually oppressive cloud anymore.

"We should do something about it," I suggested to the handful of Christian men who lived in the same city. We met once a month to pray and in the moment it seemed to me that if we all banded together, we could make a difference. I wanted the cloud gone!

"I don't know exactly what we need to do," I said, "but we could just ask the Lord and then follow His instructions."

It was one of those moments when feet shuffle and people look away. And who could blame them? We were all so far out of our comfort zone already. With no one volunteering to join me, I figured that was that. The cloud would stay.

After my initial disappointment, I rallied and decided that if I couldn't get company in this, I would just go after it alone. I know, I know. It is against the best advice of just about anyone in this space to take on territorial spirits by yourself, but unfortunately my stubbornness is over-developed and I couldn't let it go.

In any case, I climbed to a high place where I could overlook the city in the early morning light.

It was my moment of encounter.

As I stood there, I saw for the first time, the system of this world relentlessly forcing men and women to conform. It would stop at nothing to enforce its will. I saw the brokenness and woundedness of the people, their hurt and their chains. Then a portrayal of the darkness arrayed throughout the city also passed before me. It was if all the elements holding the city captive were on display—the world, the flesh and the Devil, all working together to oppress the people of the city.

I was overwhelmed, but also deeply encouraged. God had laid out what was behind the dark cloud. Surely all this revelation meant we could and would topple it.

"Okay, Lord. What should I do?"

My confidence and excitement rose. What a difference it would make for the gospel and the lives of the people when the cloud was gone . . .

Silence. I held my breath . . .

And then, the Lord brought into my mind the parable of the wheat and the tares.

I will never find words to truly describe the torrent of emotions that rushed me and in a moment beat me to my knees.

For a second the Lord had bared His soul to me, and I had glimpsed something unforgettable. He hated the cloud more than I ever could. He beheld it with perfect clarity, its tendrils tight around the lives of His beloved children. It affected Him. To Him, it was a kind of pain we could never understand, yet every day He chose to stay His hand, unwilling to root out the evil at the expense of the good and precious.

Rom 12:1-2 | Matt 13:18-22 | Matt 13:24-30

As you would expect this came with an element of frustration. Victory had seemed so close, but this was sacred ground.

For Him the end never justifies the means.

The world, the flesh and the devil . . . it was in our lives and in our families. It was in the lives of the undercover believers throughout the city. It was in the lives of the pious Muslim faithful. It was in the lives of the modern, freedom-loving people of the city as they flew their bright red colours from every other apartment balcony.

He loved us all, too much to act.

The patience and humility of God take us so far beyond human thought and comprehension.

I had come to play the hero and set things right. And though I did not get my way, I became more than a conqueror that day. I saw the heart and perspective and strategy of God, and . . . I left a worshipper.

Surprisingly I wasn't worshiping the power and might of God. He could, after all, have risen in His might to cleanse the city. Neither was it the greatness, or even the goodness, of God that left me struck with awe.

It was His patience and humility, the sheer complexity of His love and care and character, which took my breath away.

And this is what grips us most about the Cross. We didn't see it coming . . . and neither did the enemy. A heart so overrun with pride could not conceive of humility on such a scale, of using so sacrificial a means to obtain so far-reaching a victory.
God humbly stoops to walk among us. He goes even further to die and suffer in our place. The unfathomable wisdom of this outlandish victory snatched from the jaws of defeat, is founded on the Almighty's willingness to embrace levels of humility we cannot easily reconcile with deity.

Rom 8:31 | 1 Peter 3:18 | Phil 2:5-8

Q1.   What is the greatest irritant you face in life? How do you think God feels about it?

Q2.   What a privilege to glimpse the heart behind the hands we are held within. What does it mean to you in your situation if, for God, the end never justifies the means?

Q3.   What, in your world, is out of step with God's intention? How might you partner with Him in humility, determination and patience to bring change and breakthrough?

Prayer.

Lord. We pause in Your presence and let the bluster, noise and hustle of life slip away. We want to care more about the consequences, to feast on Your goodness and love. We want to know Your ways, to stand beside you, to be part of the solution rather than part of the problem. We're praying Your substantive peace and power would be released in our lives.   Amen.

CHAPTER TEN

DIVINE FAVOUR

WE HAD ONE OF THOSE WEIRD CONVERSATIONS
YOU HAVE WHEN ONE PERSON IS ON THE PHONE
AND THE OTHER IS LISTENING IN.

We'd been in Turkey less than a week, seven of us, squeezed into a tiny two-room apartment in a city five hours north of the one we had planned to settle in. All our well-laid plans for Izmir had evaporated just days before we had boarded our scheduled flights.

Then, with just one phone call, some friends offered us the use of their place for the seven weeks they were away on holiday. Sure, it was in another city, but at least now we had a plan B. We would go there instead, and I would travel to Izmir ahead of my family and get things sorted once again. Seven weeks seemed enough. It wasn't optimal but it was doable, so we boarded the plane from Brisbane to Istanbul.

The first week in Turkey was surreal. Our bodies and souls were time-torn between an old life a world away and a whole new reality. But our sleep, the only real answer to jet-lag, was shattered by a call to prayer so loud the eloquent muezzin could have been in our bedroom. In fact, there were so many mosques per square foot in Bursa's old city, he nearly was!

Somewhere between slumber and the moment of wakefulness, I heard the voice of God.

"I've uncovered your feet."

"What?"

Now I was awake.

"I've uncovered your feet."

I tried to understand but I got no further, because suddenly the day erupted with activity.

Too many people and so many suitcases in such a limited space—it was all haste and chaos to have breakfast and get out the door. We were off to visit a real estate agent, an uninvited interruption to our plans.

We had visited Bursa, Izmir and Istanbul a few months earlier, and had promptly ruled out Bursa as a potential city to live in. It was like the cultural divide was a bridge too far. Istanbul was a more obvious choice for Westerners, but it was also uber-busy. You took your life in your hands just to cross a road there. How would we cope with a large family and such young children? Making a life for our family in Istanbul, we decided, was also untenable.

We had settled on Izmir.

But the day before, an Australian woman who had met us in Istanbul and guided us to Bursa, phoned Anya.

"I spoke with my real estate agent this morning," she said, "and she has some houses for you to look at if you think you might want to stay here in Bursa. If you like, I can come over with her tomorrow morning and take you to see them."

This was not what we wanted. On that we were agreed, but the tinge of hope in her voice made Anya hesitate.

We had one of those weird conversations when one person is on the phone and the other isn't, and, with an intermittently muffled microphone, a few charades and the depth of unspoken conversation and gestured cues effective only at such times, we agreed to go.

We could only imagine how lonely and isolated their family must have felt. There were hardly any foreigners in Bursa, at least, of our variety, and for good reason. I guess we unconsciously decided to humour them a little. After all, why not take a look?

And so, Anya said "Yes" on our behalf, and now, here we were, hurrying everyone out the door.

Our family piled into the car with Ros and the real estate agent. Seatbelts and seating capacity are a sort of optional extra in Turkey, which of course has its plusses and minuses for a family of six unable to usually fit into a medium sized car.

"I've got three houses to show you," the agent said as we started off.

The next hour turned us upside down.

House number one was perfect!

An old man greeted kids with cherries from his tree. There was a playground across the road. It was clean, fresh, bright and modern, and surrounded by lush grass, which is not something to be taken for granted there.

Unexpectedly, we actually could imagine ourselves making a home there.

Before we knew it, we were perched on seats outside the real estate agent's office, drinking tea and expressing our surprise at how things had come to this.

In the middle of a stilted and confused conversation between the two of us, I suddenly recalled what God had said a few hours before.

"I've uncovered your feet."

And in a flash, we knew what the Lord had meant.

It was from the story of Ruth. When she crept close in the darkness and uncovered Boaz's feet it meant something quite specific . . .

"I want you to do Me a favour." Only now it wasn't Ruth asking a favour of Boaz. It was God asking something of us!

Ruth 3:7-13

"Would you do Me a favour and live in Bursa?"

We understood the request. It made sense. The other Aussie/Kiwi family with children of a similar age could use some company. God had led us to Turkey. He was quite within His rights to choose the city as well, regardless of our initial preference.

What was more difficult to grasp was the language He had used. When does God ever ask for favours from people?

The truth is, we would have grudgingly agreed, had He instructed us to live in Bursa. Instead, the tenor of His request was so humble and warm. It was entirely irresistible. 'Would you do Me a favour?'

We agreed.

We said, "Yes."

From the moment we signed the lease on that property, Bursa became our city, and our home. It was as though something huge had shifted in our hearts.

To this day the city and its people remain dear to us.

God came to us humbly, and we changed our posture to match his. He had won our hearts through a demonstration of His own.

The next two years were phenomenal. God swept us up in what He was doing.

Since then, Anya has written a book about our time there. It's called, "Foreigners in the City of Silk." When I read it, when I think back to those years, it is nearly heart-breaking to imagine that we could have missed the opportunity to live in Bursa.

And we are so grateful for the way God got His message through to us. Somehow, it seemed to require humility both on His part and ours to make it happen.

Q1.   What word has the Lord spoken to you or over you that shocked and confused you at the time?

Q2.   Are we in a position to hinder or forbid God when He wants to release His intention for us into our life?

Q3.   Do you find God guiding you through any low doorways in your life right now, challenging your desires and/or your theology?

Prayer.

Lord. We'd rather know You than fit You into our flimsy boxes. You don't live in buildings made with hands, yet You are found in the highest heights and the lowest depths. Like Moses, we turn aside to look at an incomprehensible revelation of Your glory and we stoop to unfasten our shoes. Barefoot and curious, we revel in the one who is more than we will ever truly know.   Amen.

CHAPTER ELEVEN

NEIGHBOURS

WHAT IS TRANSACTED IN HUMILITY IS ENACTED WITH EVER WIDENING AUTHORITY AND INFLUENCE AS HE RAISES US.

Not long after we arrived in New Zealand, Anya and I applied for a job as pastors of a church. Through a confluence of events we found ourselves open to the role and began to invest in the church community. Although the recruitment process took forever—nine months of our life we will never get back—we enjoyed ministering to the people as we waited. In fact, we became comfortable to the point where we began to think it might just turn out!

Somewhere along the line, however, I met another couple who had applied for the same job. They were awesome. And somehow, the fact that we were in competition for the role got to me a bit. Later that day, I retreated into a nearby nature reserve to hike and chat it over with the Lord.

"What's going on? Why does this bother me so much?"

Right away, He directed me to the words of Jesus. "Love the Lord your God with all your heart . . . and love your neighbour as yourself."

It seemed as though He was in coach mode. He wanted me to adopt a good attitude towards the other couple, to express positivity and love toward them, in spite of the fact that we were in competition.

As I tramped up a giant set of stairs, the exertion cleared my head and calmed my nerves. I chanted the words repeatedly as I ascended . . .

Matt 22:37-39

"Love the Lord your God . . ."

"With all your heart and mind and strength . . ."

"Love your neighbour as yourself . . ."

I kept on until I was about halfway towards the summit, where I stopped to rest and reflect on one of those well-placed seats on the trail.

It was as I sat there that God released a gentle revelation into my heart. He wanted to interpret His word for me . . .

God loved the other candidate for the job as much as He loved me. He wanted the other party blessed as much as He wanted to bless us and our family. His love for them was as great as His love for me. My self-centred thinking about the selection process actually put me out of step with God's mind. To stay the course I needed to humble myself and bring my heart into alignment with God's. When I love my neighbour as myself, my attitude matches his.

My brain buzzed as I digested this idea. This was the antidote to my inner conflict! As I applied my realisation not just to the couple I had met, but to all humanity, I began to perceive God's love for all people everywhere on earth regardless of their eternal destination, ethnicity, gender, creed or religion. He loves us all perfectly and without limitation, and though so much stands in the way of His desires for us, His heart is enlarged toward us all. He is for *us*— every one of us.

The truth is, if humility were universal, it would fix the world. Humility on a global scale would bring an end to war, famine, corporate greed, and every other outcome of an oppressive mindset.

Or, to put it another way, if we were all to humble ourselves and seek His face, He would heal our land—all our lands; He could and would heal the entire world!

So where is the point of difference? If His love is the same toward all, why does humanity experience such a variety in terms of blessing, revelation of truth and intimacy with the Lord?

2 Chron 7:14

It comes down to our response to His meekly presented invitation as He welcomes us into our destiny. Will we affirm His word over our life?

Will we take off our shoes? Will we fall to our knees, casting ourselves at His feet as prostrate worshippers? Our worship invites His presence! He meets us down there on the floor! He is content to stoop. He has the low-down on the down-low—he knows the payoff is incredible. When we sow humility, we reap honour. As God raises us up to walk before him, we begin to receive an ever-widening sphere of authority and influence, blessing and favour.

Now the seeds of our destiny can take root, allowing us to live out His desire for our lives, unlocking benefit for those around us, and drawing out in us who we were really made to be.

Humility positions us to enter into the desires of His heart. In the Father's house a banquet is laid. His desire is for every seat to be filled, and as we rise to accept His invitation, a glad smile breaks out on His face.

Paul's letter to the Ephesians shows His perfect will. The equality of His love and intended treatment for every person on earth is matched by a similar attitude expressed in the heavenlies. Everyone who breaks through to enjoy His love there is accepted in Christ. In the heavenlies, *everyone* receives *every* spiritual blessing. In the spiritual realm, everyone who turns up gets it all!

The problem is not lack of divine resources and or lack of inclination in the heart of God. The problem behind unrealised destinies and people living outside all that God intends for them, is human pride.

On earth, pride wears heavy boots designed to stomp over others—anything to climb, or achieve budgets or reach goals. Pride's children are oppressive. Pride takes more than needed. It pillages long-term resources for short term gain. Pride opens its mouth with threats of violence. It causes the weak to cower in fear. Pride destroys family and community. It strips away independence, identity and dignity. It leaves us desolate, dispossessed, disappointed, depressed, fearful, isolated and alone. Pride, in line with its originator's character, steals, kills and destroys. Pride has ruined this planet and humility is the only antidote.

1 Cor 15:43 | Eph 1-2

Heaven, on the other hand, overflows with beauty, abundance, comfort and wonder. Pride cannot steal it away or destroy it, but it can keep us from ever turning towards our heavenly home. With its endless stream of excuses, pride can hinder or delay us from entering. Pride can never change the truth that yes, there is enough and to spare in our Father's house. Yet pride can distract us so we never heed the invitation, so that we never stoop, so that we never enter in.

Prostrate worshippers, however, are graced to cast off pride. They hear His voice. They enter to enjoy His lavish and abundant blessings. Their cup overflows and they come out of the heavenlies full and armoured up, bringing more than enough of heaven to sate the pain of a pride-ravished world.

Luke 15:17 | John 10:3-4 | Heb 4:1 | Ps 23:5 | Eph 6:10-17

Q1.   How do you go with reconciling God's universally benevolent heart with the wide disparities and inequities in this world—wealth and want, blessing and desperation?

Q2.   Who is your neighbour? Who in your life right now needs to experience the love of God to the level you have enjoyed it?

Q3.   Who do you consider more an object of God's love than yourself, and who do you feel intuitively is less important to Him than you? What would you do or say differently if you "loved them as yourself"?

Prayer.

Lord. You love perfectly and without measure. We long for Your attention and favour, and in this moment choose to renounce the toxicity of competition. We still ourselves in Your presence and allow You to quiet us with Your love. We affirm Your lavish desire toward all of Your children and climb onto the altar again, so as living sacrifices we might cast off selfish and bitter restraints and learn to love again, to love a world full of hurt and need.   Amen.

HERO WORSHIP

Jesus, knowing that the Father had given all things into His hands, and that He had come from God and was going to God, rose from supper and laid aside His garments, took a towel and girded Himself. After that, He poured water into a basin and began to wash the disciples' feet, and to wipe them with the towel with which He was girded.

John 13:3-5

Jacob Wrestling with the Angel

Now that we have established humility as a fundamental facet of the character of God, let's turn to explore the backstory of God. An ancient tale recounts a collision of pride and humility—a prideful villain set against a humble God. The glory of heaven became a defiled war-torn ruin, until a hero rose to check the rebellion. Humility overcame, and the rogue and his followers were cast down, banished from paradise.

But the story of the Hero and the villain doesn't end there.

It's as if God has embedded His story into all of ours. In fact, it seems to be intrinsically woven into the fabric of creation; now, a path of righteousness and another of wickedness are set before us all. They come to us as two scripts. Will we play the hero, or will we take the villain's part?

Come with me back in time, before creation, before history, before the beginning. Come and stand beside a humble God as He grapples with the suffering, loss, pain and rejection He has experienced. Let's find perspective for when our stories begin to sound the same. Could it be that my low points, the grief and discomfort I sometimes face in life, somehow retell His story? Could our difficulties be an exercise in intimately echoing the story of God. Could they be an opportunity for Him to make Himself known more fully to us?

We are being invited into the script of His life—a script that draws us into humility, then powerfully takes us from our lowly position into eternal glory and exaltation in Christ. As we align to His story, that guarantees a similar trajectory and end for our tale as well.

Join me as we explore the story of the Hero and the villain . . .

PART

2

THE HERO AND
THE VILLAIN

HERO WORSHIP

In the beginning was the Word, and the Word was with God, and the Word was God. He was in the beginning with God. All things were made through Him, and without Him nothing was made that was made. In Him was life, and the life was the light of men. And the light shines in the darkness, and the darkness did not comprehend it.

John 1:1-5

Death of Samson

CHAPTER TWELVE

GOD'S BACKSTORY

WAR-TORN CLAMOUR DROWNS OUT AND
INTERRUPTS THE RHYTHMS OF
CEASELESS WORSHIP.

Neil Diamond croons over his "Sweet Caroline." It's a song about the joy of intimacy, and though it might not be entirely PG in its sentiments, it came to mind as I contemplated the message of this book.

He delights in her . . . he calls her name out loud, over and over.

> *Good times never seemed so good . . .*
> *Look at the night and it don't seem so lonely . . .*
> *And when I hurt*
> *Hurting runs off my shoulders*
> *How can I hurt when I'm holding you?*

As we listen, we sense that behind the joy in his girl there is also a backstory, a history of hurt and disappointment.

All is not well with him—but then, "Sweet Caroline" comes into his life, and with her comes radical change. The narrative shifts. Pain loses its grip. Joy breaks through disillusionment like the sunrise at dawn.

Life has not become picture perfect; instead, someone special has come and changed the flavour of his life.

God has a backstory, too.

He has lived through times of pain and heartache.

When we experience difficult times, when we look up to heaven in disbelief or even angrily shake our fist skyward, it seldom enters our mind that heaven might understand.

Who knew that God had first-hand experience of pain and heartache?

In our troubles, we put our head down, grit our teeth and push through. "This too shall pass," we mumble to ourselves as we pray, amidst cold hard realities.

The rugged earth seems far removed from the scenes of celestial splendour.

"God. How about a hand down here?"

A metallic clang—our words rebound off a brazen heaven.

"No night there. No tears there. No darkness or pain either. How could heaven possibly understand?"

 "He understands."

"Sure. His infinite mind understands everything, but I doubt He gets what it *feels* like. I'm not an academic exercise, an object of study or a math problem."

"He doesn't just understand. He gets it too."

"What can He possibly be aware of that's even close to what I have gone through?"

"He has lived long. He too has suffered loss, betrayal and pain."

God has a backstory, too.

Heaven, His home, has been a battleground—its joy rent by civil war, brother pitched against brother, angels once allies, now bitter enemies.

A catastrophic clash of might decimates the former glory of a paradise caught in the crossfire. War-torn clamour drowns out and interrupts the rhythms of ceaseless worship.

Rev 21:4 | Rev 22:3-4

Heaven is in ruins, groaning under the weight of immense loss, birthed out of an intimate betrayal.

Do you feel the heartache of God? Perfect love created the highest and most glorious of all His angelic friends. Perfect love embraced and honoured Lucifer to rule His heaven . . . perfect love, without self-protection or reserve.

But perfect love was cut to ribbons by duplicity, pride and the greatest overreach of all time.

It was a messy divorce if ever there was one.

Then, someone replaces the traitor, someone whose love is as pure as the Father's.

He is just and true and anointed.

The rebuild of heaven begins. Peacetime remains elusive, yet the arrival of the anointed one is transformative to the atmosphere. All He touches goes as it should. The disappointment and pain associated with the deficient-one pales with every thought, every word, and every action of the one who dispossessed him.

Jesus, Sweet Jesus!

We invoke the name not only to get tasks accomplished in the spirit. We speak it because we love him. He is the anointed one who has taken our brokenness and dismay and remade it into something wonderful.

My beloved Son! Heaven rends as the Father steps up to the portal between His world and ours. Having seen it all, He is compelled to speak. With ecstatic acclaim He interrupts Christ's baptism and transfiguration. *I'm pleased with this one.*

We and the Father are united in the moment: we all have a backstory and Christ the Son has made it all okay—better than okay! We all can't get enough of Jesus!

I never picked up on this previously, that the Father's pleasure over His Son didn't begin with His incarnation. In the backstory of God, Jesus has always

1 John 4:18 | 1 John 4:8 | John 14:14 | Matt 3:17 | Matt 17:5 | John 12:28

played the hero of the story. He dispossessed the villain and soothed the pain of Lucifer's betrayal. This was not the first time the Father had gushed over His beloved Son.

Neil sings another refrain of "Sweet Caroline."

And we join heaven as the praises of Jesus ring out. He's responsible for the transformation . . . beauty for ashes . . . The oil of joy for mourning . . . and a garment of praise for the spirit of heaviness. The Father joins in. The lyrics of His song and the notes He reaches as He sings in delight over His Son leave us full of wonderment.

Two trees stood in the Garden of Eden. Two, surrounded by many, testifying to another Eden in another place where the Father and Son dwelt amid the angelic host.

Christ's tree is the "tree of life." All He does is redemptive and life-giving.

The other tree represents the Father. How does He identify Himself?

"I'm the one who has experienced both agony and ecstasy. I'm the one with the knowledge of both good and evil. I've known two intimate companions and they were poles apart—one wounded Me deeply, and the other was My greatest joy."

God has a backstory.

Isa 61:3 | Gen 2:15-17

Q1.   Consider Lucifer's betrayal and God's backstory and then reflect on your own situation. What specifically comes to mind about your story that God might understand more than you originally thought?

Q2.   Who would you see as the hero of the tale when it comes to your life? Looking back, who has made things right for you along the way?

Q3.   In what way do you see Christ as your hero? What, in your experience of him, draws you to worship?

Prayer.

Lord. You are our saviour, redeemer, our righteousness and the one who has lifted up our heads and hearts. Christ, we worship You as the answer to our every desire and need. We reflect on what life was before we knew You. What a difference You have made in our life—we are left in quiet adoration. We praise You. You are our all in all, our sweet Jesus. We choose to align ourselves with Your rule and reign. With You as Lord of our lives we know we will fulfil our destinies and live life to the full.   Amen.

CHAPTER THIRTEEN

PRIDE VS. HUMILITY

A FORMLESS, NAMELESS MASS OF HUMANITY
BAYING FOR BLOOD, DRIVEN ON BY THE
DARKNESS, COULD NOT GET THE JOB DONE.

Night fell, and everyone went to their own homes. Except Jesus. Jesus went to the Mount of Olives. It was His hangout place with the Father—tonight, this time of connecting together was pivotal, given what dawn's light would bring. The religious leaders would soon arrive with a test for Jesus, a trap. Driven by the one who will use any means to achieve an end, they had enticed a woman into an illicit act and then humiliated and accused her.

She was simply bait to them—the woman caught in adultery.

Jesus was their intended prey.

The trap was founded on the tension between their Jewish religious law and the regulations imposed by the Roman secular state.

Jesus must choose between two legal systems in conflict with one another— one civil, one religious. He's being set up to fail. The Accuser is amidst the crowd longing to focus his attention on the Saviour. The woman is irrelevant to him. The destroyer lurks, thirstily preying upon the Son of God.

The trap is sprung. There's no way out this time.

But Jesus had been with the Father. He had spent the night in the presence of humility itself.

John 7:53-8:6

In His father's heart, the means never justifies the end; in His heart dwells an relentless determination to achieve redemptive purposes regardless of the context.

The Father sees and knows in the spirit. He sees the darkness and the light. He knows the way of the enemy and He knows Christ. He has knowledge of good and evil. Lucifer sees the mob as a mass of potential to use for his own ends. The Father sees each individual; He knows their names and is familiar with the story of every life.

The Father speaks a word and that word will not rest until its work is done. That day, His immutable word would find a home in each and every soul in the crowd.

> He was determined to save and honour His Son.

> He was determined to speak into the lives of every accuser.

> He was determined to redeem the life of the nameless woman.

When Jesus speaks, He is echoing the words of His father:

"Let the one who is without sin cast the first stone."

The crowd ebbs until only Jesus and the woman remain.

The Law was explicit.

> Roman law said . . .

>> that Jews could not take matters into their own hands.

> Jewish law said . . .

>> that she should die for this kind of behaviour;

>> and that two or more witnesses were required. They must cast the first stone. The witnesses must lead the way in the administration of justice.

The truth was, no one wanted their name on this. To have come forward as a witness would have put them in the centre of the trap they had meant for Christ.

Isa 55:11 | John 8:7-10 | John 18:31 | Lev 20:10 | Deut 17:6-7 | Deut 19:15-18

So, they drifted away.

With everyone gone, with no-one to stand beside him, without the presence of two or three witnesses, Jesus could not legally stone the woman either.

The Father had brought Him into a legally defensible posture of mercy.

"Where are your accusers?" He asks. Then He says to the woman, "Neither do I condemn you. Go and sin no more."

It was as legally impeccable as the cross and our redemption.

The wisdom of God and the power of God—relentless and determined humility.

A formless, nameless mass of humanity baying for blood, driven on by the darkness, could not overcome this life-changing power. Relentless humility prevailed. Redemptive purposes prevailed. The light shone into the darkness and the darkness took a step back, unable to comprehend it.

But Jesus had only one point of focus. He would ensure the Father received all the credit for His words and actions.

"I see Him . . . I hear Him . . . and I speak."

The hero of this story is entirely humble. Without hesitation He deflects the glory of His victory towards the Father.

We don't usually associate humility and heroism, but it works somehow here.

In the Son of God, humility and heroism have come together. It is suggestive of a practiced ease in this stance. It is His true identity.

He has been the humble hero all His eternal life!

John 8:10-11 | John 1:5 | John 8:26-29, 38 | John 5:17-20

Q1.   What does it mean to you to emulate Christ's humble heroism?

Q2.   Where do you direct the credit when you achieve something significant?

Q3.   Christ's stance in the face of the religious set allowed Him to succeed. What was His unfair advantage? Could his approach inform your responses in similarly tricky situations?

Prayer.

Lord. We thank You for a connection to heaven and ask to be graced to hear Your voice and see You at work in our lives. We want to be able to respond in kind. Make us vessels of Your grace and power, able to walk free of carnality and any religious spirit so as to bring hope to the accused, the broken and downtrodden. Help us to walk as Jesus walked.   Amen.

CHAPTER FOURTEEN

TWO SCRIPTS

ONE SCRIPT DEFINES WICKEDNESS.
THE OTHER DESCRIBES THOSE
KNOWN AS 'THE RIGHTEOUS ONES.'

Humility works for God. It is who He is—and it's how He comes at situations. And while His unexpectedly humble bearing seems more than enough perspective for us to reflect on for years to come, there is something more . . .

God is humble, *and* He always has been.

This is important.

In the backstory of God, well before creation, God was humble. In fact, when God crafted the world, humility was so much a part of His character that He wove it into the very fabric of creation. It's as if the world we live in is set up to provide an unfair advantage to those who are humble; it supports those who share His character . . . those who possess humility.

There is grace—favour—for the humble.

God gives grace to the humble.

What if creation was more than a pragmatic act, forming a backdrop for God's redemptive purposes? What if creation is best understood as an artistic retelling, the portrayal of a narrative dear to His heart?

In His backstory, there was something beautiful and delightful that characterised His son—humility!

James 4:6 | 1 Peter 5:5-6

He, the Hero, shared the same humble heart as His father, bringing Him immense joy. Along the way, He dispossessed the villain who was, in complete contrast, riddled with pride.

God designed the world to favour those who are like the Hero and to oppose those who are like the villain.

In other words, there are two scripts—the hero script and the villain script.

One is the definition of wickedness. The others are known as the righteous.

Humility is the ultimate key to virtue and an upright life; pride is at the core of all iniquity and depravity.

The two scripts are described in biblical wisdom literature as a choice of two paths, one leading to life and the other to destruction; or, as two women: Wisdom and Folly. Which will you and I embrace?

Moses says, "I set before you life and death. Chose life."

The choice is always two-fold. Which script do we prefer? Will we play the part of the villain or the Hero?

Recently, a verse caught my attention. I memorised it because it captures the cause and effect of humility in a nearly mathematical way:

> *By humility and the fear of the Lord are riches and honor and life.*

Humility + the Fear of the Lord = Riches and Honour and Life.

Whether it is our relationships, our health or our bank balance, humility is the key to success and a lifestyle of favour.

Who knew?

Until this season of my life, I never realised the vital place humility has in the order of things. It permeates scripture, though I had never seen it. For example:

> *. . . what does the Lord require of you, but to do justly, to love mercy, and to walk humbly with your God?*

Prov 4:18-19 | Prov 9 | Deut 30:15-20 | Prov 22:4

And, this one, which captures the entire narrative of the Hero and the villain in a single simple saying:

> *God resists the proud, but gives grace to the humble.*

Again, and again the theme is recited. Humility seems to be everywhere . . .

> *Therefore humble yourselves under the mighty hand of God, that*
> *He may exalt you in due time.*

Why? Because there was an original hero and an original villain, and the two primeval scripts that recount their respective tales are the basis for all the cause and effect within the created order.

Humility leads to success. It feels counter-intuitive—until we grasp the truth that *all creation honours the Son.*

Humility leads to riches, honour and a long life, and the human heart senses the need of these. We don't get it. We think only of ourselves and climb over one another in our haste to advance and attain them, but a proud, selfish or combative spirit do not lead upward because . . .

> *Pride goes before destruction, and a haughty spirit before a fall. Better to be of*
> *a humble spirit with the lowly, than to divide the spoil with the proud.*

Those who oppress others to get ahead themselves are going about things the wrong way entirely. Jesus said, in His Sermon on the Mount,

> *Blessed are the meek, for they shall inherit the earth.*

Who knew? Invisible forces are at work behind the scenes and only when we understand how they are wired to the hero and the villain scripts can we make sense of the wisdom of Christ when He declared,

> *. . . the last will be first, and the first last.*

The last dispossessed the first. The humble Hero rose to pre-eminence, and the prideful villain, in the end, lost his place, his position and all his property.

Micah 6:8 | Prov 3:34 | James 4:6 | 1 Peter 5:5-6 | Prov 16:18-19 | Matt 5:5 | Matt 20:16

Q1.   Reflect on your character. How would you grade yourself on a continuum between pride and humility, and on what basis would you choose your score?

Pride - 1 2 3 4 5 6 7 8 9 10 - Humility

Q2.   This chapter suggests we are faced with a black and white decision between two scripts rather than an array of choice along a continuum. Given this perspective which script do you find yourself on?

Q3.   Do you intuitively affirm scripture's suggestion that humility is fundamental to success in life? Is it more difficult for you to embrace humility or do you find any desire to be blessed in this life problematic and unable to be reconciled with your faith?

Prayer.

Lord. You are wisdom and Your mind and heart is wonderful to us. We embrace humility, who You are and the long journey You have been on. We ask You to take us in hand to quench and quell our rebel heart—reshape us into conformity and gift us with Your mind. Diffuse our obsession with ourselves, until we find ourselves re-centred into Your story—lost in you, Lord Jesus.   Amen.

CHAPTER FIFTEEN

DISPOSSESSION

SCRIPTURE BURSTS OPEN UNTIL WE SEE
THE FATHER AS MUCH LESS ELUSIVE
THAN WE PREVIOUSLY BELIEVED.

After Saul died, David took his position and place. That kind of thing happens a lot in scripture; his is just one of a multitude of examples of dispossession taking place within the circumstances of real-life people within those pages.

As if that isn't enough, there is more to the pattern. As it turns out, there are *three* characters found in the dispossession scenarios of the Bible.

We know the first two—the Hero and the villain. The other is the Father. Father God was betrayed by Lucifer (the villain) and the Son stepped in to dispossess him, filling the void that was left after his fall. We could portray it like this:

FATHER

~~Villain~~   ←Hero

One did everything well and delighted the Father. The other deeply wounded him. And the two are in conflict with each other.

Who will take the place closest to the Father?

The pattern is repeated . . .

Let's look at Saul and David again.

1 Sam 16:1-14, 15:28

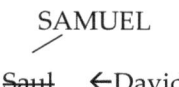

SAMUEL

~~Saul~~ ←David

After Saul died, David took his position and place. Samuel takes the role of the Father. He becomes a reference point around which the dispossession of Saul and the rise of David takes place. The hero shines so bright. The role is not without difficulty, but the hero always triumphs in the end. Consider Samuel's pleasure with David as he stands in complete contrast with Saul's disobedience and rebellion. The Hero takes the throne to another level. He dispossesses and perfectly surpasses the villain, while the Father's heart is satisfied . . .

The same dynamics are at play when Vashti, the queen, spurns king Xerxes and finds herself dispossessed, replaced by Esther.

XERXES

~~Vashti~~ ←Esther

Think of Esther, beautiful and noble, forgetful of herself, yet faithful to her people. She values her place and position, unlike her predecessor Vashti, who gave it all away on a whim. Two women, one playing the hero, the other the villain. Of all the women in the selection process, only one delights the heart of King Xerxes.

The retelling speaks of the rich extent to which the Son delighted the Father in that time of His exploits before history or creation!

Suddenly, we realise that scripture bursts with pictures of the Father and these two, the Hero and the villain, as they contend to be His closest companion. Maybe the Father is less elusive in scripture than we previously believed.

If we keep Xerxes as the central figure, the story is repeated by Mordechai and Haman. Mordechai dispossesses Haman, taking his place and position of authority before Xerxes.

XERXES

~~Haman~~ ←Mordechai

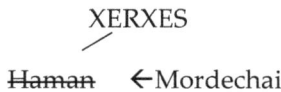

1 Sam 13:13-14 | Esther 1:1-2:18 | Esther 8:2

Mordechai is glorious. His heart is for Xerxes and the kingdom. He is faithful and just and true. Despite Haman's threats, he brings him to and end and dispossesses him.

He is honoured by the king (a moment retold again in the Triumphal Entry of Christ and the ascent of Solomon to the throne).

Mordechai, right on script, rises majestically to usher in a new and glorious era.

ISAAC

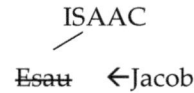

~~Esau~~   ←Jacob

The same is true for Isaac and his two sons, one of whom plays the hero, the other, following the script of the villain. Jacob, the brother who seemed to be in second place, ends up with Esau's inheritance. How can he be a thief and still be a hero? Isn't it because he dispossessed his brother, the one who came before, and replayed the part of the Hero in the original primeval script? Isn't it because his brother thought so little of his position and place as the eldest son, and his right to inherit all of the blessings in Abraham's line? Isaac gives all he has to Jacob and for Esau there is nothing left at all. In the end, villainy has no reward!

DAVID

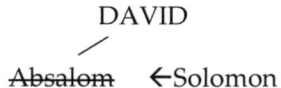

~~Absalom~~   ←Solomon

David is a special case. After he becomes king, his role changes, as if he's changes script midway.

Earlier he played the hero, with Saul as the villain; later in life he plays the Father, while Solomon is the hero and Absalom plays the villain.

And so his heart breaks as Absalom rises and tries to take it all. Another intimate betrayal. Absalom humiliates and even tries to kill David, causing David to flee for his life, effectively losing his people, his kingdom and his crown overnight.

After his death, however, Absalom is replaced by Solomon. Solomon is the faithful son, and under his reign a glorious era like none other is established.

Esther 6 ǀ 1 Kings 1:32-40 ǀ Gen 27 ǀ 2 Sam 15-18 ǀ 1 Kings 9-10

ABRAHAM
/
~~Ishmael~~   ←Isaac

Consider Isaac, the legitimate son and heir who takes the place of Ishmael, the one who Abraham is adamant will not walk away with the inheritance. The pattern of dispossession continues. Isaac takes it all.

POTIPHER
/
~~Potiphar's wife~~   ←Joseph

Then there's Potiphar, so enamoured with Joseph and his faithfulness. In contrast, his wife's unfaithfulness cuts him to the core. Her betrayal is two-fold. Her barbed duplicity sees Potiphar reel in anger and jealous frustration, and also finds Joseph condemned to accusation and prison.

Joseph's story continues. The betrayer is in his past. Pharaoh takes over from Potiphar in the role of the Father. He has gained the highest place and no villain opposes him now. Joseph stands beside the king and rules the entire kingdom. He has answers to the bitter threat of famine, and under his hand the kingdom goes from strength to strength.

Every time his story is retold, the villain overreaches, struggles, falls and fails, never to recover their previous place.

As we read, sometimes we feel repulsion towards those who play this part, other times pity seems appropriate. Potiphar's wife. Yuk! What a sleaze! And, in terms of intimate betrayal, Delilah is without equal. Sensual and untrue, so easily bought for a price—Samson's world literally collapses as the one he trusted turned against him.

All these Bible characters in their ordinary lives begin to tell an incredible tale— the backstory of God. It occurred centuries or maybe eons before creation.

Who can show us what Father God is like? Those who play His part—Samuel, King Xerxes, Isaac, Potiphar, Pharaoh, and King David all teach us of the one who tends to remain in the background of scripture.

Gen 25:5-6 I **Gen 39** I **Gen 41** I **Gen 39:11-18** I **Judges 16**

What can we know of the beloved pre-incarnate Son of God prior to creation and His role as Jehovah and our Saviour Jesus Christ? David in his early life, Esther, Mordechai, Isaac, Joseph, Jacob, and Solomon all play the part of the Hero, as they dispossess their rivals. They are a vivid portrayal of humility, character and eventual greatness and glory. They define righteousness and wisdom and show us how to live well.

And then there are the motley crew who show us the opposite—Saul, Vashti, Haman, Ishmael, Potiphar's wife, Esau, Absalom, Delilah and Judas . . . each play the part of the villain. Why is that? To demonstrate the consequences of pride, wrong values and poor choices. Their story shows us what *not* to do!

At first glance this may disturb us; it feels uncanny.

Do we all just play a part, pawns in a cosmic game or players on a celestial stage? Is there any free will at all?

The answer is, "Yes."

We do get to decide, but in the end there are really only two choices—two scripts and two pathways.

When you make your choice, each step you take begins to draw you towards the natural conclusion of either the original Hero or the villain. We are propelled toward the end result of the particular script we choose.

You act like the Hero and are carried towards blessing and success.

You emulate the villain, perhaps with little realisation of what this even means, and your association with him quickly drags you towards a ruin akin to what he experienced.

The choice is yours!

Q1.   Choose one or more of the on-script heroes listed in this chapter. Which would you most like to emulate? What qualities catch your eye?

Q2.   Which of the villains in scripture could you easily become if you let yourself go?

Q3.   Being on-script, is a question of character and heart rather than behaviour. What New Testament principles, perspectives or approaches help us with this?

Prayer.

Lord. We treasure our inheritance and reach for it. Before you, we forsake this present world for so much more. Grace us to be faithful to You and Your people, to value our place in Your plans. Keep us so we do not sell our souls against the needs of the moment. Draw out nobility in us. Whenever we fall, stumble or feel offence, plant in us courage and resolve; grant us a deep filling of faith, hope and determination, and an eagerness to see Your story retold in our lives, as it was in the greats who have gone before us. Amen.

CHAPTER SIXTEEN

THE ACTUAL HERO

JESUS EMBRACED THE ROLE. ROBBED
OF ALL DIGNITY AND SOUNDLY
REJECTED, HE SWAPPED PARTS WITH US.

How can a person compose and sing soulful psalms one day, and demonstrate brawny prowess on the battlefield the next? David managed both. He fought innumerable battles, yet is most fondly remembered for his compilation of emotive praise anthems and vulnerable songs of worship—the book of Psalms.

King David is a vivid picture (or type) of God the Father. Both are described as 'singing warriors,' mighty on one hand, and melodious and tender on the other. The following verse gives us a glimpse of this in relation to God:

The Lord your God in your midst, the Mighty One, will save; He will rejoice over you with gladness, He will quiet you with His love, He will rejoice over you with singing.

The similarities between the two continue to play out in their parenting.

David's relationships with two of his sons, Absalom and Solomon, offer rich reflections on fatherhood; but critically both relationships reveal something of the story, character and heart of Father God.

Let's bring David's two very different sons onto the stage, into the spotlight. One is glorious and a credit to his father in all his accomplishments; the otherturns against David and betrays him, seizing his kingdom, forcing him into exile and humiliating him entirely.

2 Sam 22 | Zeph 3:17 | 1 Kings 9-10 | 2 Sam 15-18

The rebel son comes to his inevitable end—a lone figure, hanging on a tree— as his father, David, weeps inconsolably in the background.

Traditionally, we see Absalom as a picture pointing forward to Jesus' death on a 'tree.' It's easy to correlate the Father with King David—both overwhelmed by grief as their sons hang from their respective trees.

The connection is there, and it's real.

Still, there is something shocking about the sudden realisation that Jesus, the perfect Son of God, and Absalom, the villain in King David's story, are so eerily alike in the death.

It messes with our minds.

Both encounter the same, shameful end. Death on a tree.

And yet, Jesus was so vividly like David's other son as well. Like Solomon He rides triumphantly into Jerusalem, recognised and loved by the people, the hope of the nation. Solomon too, is known for his glorious reign.

The scandal of the cross, with its pain, mocking and shame, collides with an exemplary life that stirs the hearts of the multitude and draws forth heaven's affirmation. Christ brings together two opposing streams of biblical imagery.

Sometimes He's like Haman, hung up in death and shame; other times, like Mordechai, faithful and magnificent.

Scripture resounds with connections to Jesus—*Christ in all the scriptures.*

But, here is a question I never felt to ask before . . .

> *Does all scripture prophetically point forward to Jesus, the incarnate Son?*

It's true that in thirty-three years He blew our minds, stole our hearts, defeated the darkness and turned our world upside down.

But let's for a moment face in the other direction. What if scripture points *backwards* to Christ instead? What if the scriptures primarily testify to the 'glory He had before the world was'—as the original and glorious champion of

2 Sam 18:11-33 | 1 Peter 2:24 | 1 Kings 1:33 | John 12:12-15 | Esther 7:9-10 | John 17

heaven at a time when the kingdom of God was fraught and beset with violence and oppression?

Even when He comes in flesh, joining the cast of biblical heroes as a character on the sacred page, His humiliation echoes His ancient past.

It all comes down to our point of view.

Such a drastic shift in perspective is reminiscent of a theory held by the renowned scientist, Nicolaus Copernicus, when he proposed that our planet rotated around the Sun, not the sun around the earth. It was a radically new perspective, and widely opposed. Surely if the planet Earth was the setting for creation, the incarnation, and redemption—the home of the people of God— then it must also be the astronomical centre too.

Over time, however, his outlandish theory became mainstream. Nowadays we understand that earth is not really the astronomical centre of much at all!

Importantly, when Copernicus changed the reference point, the models and math involved in the physics of planetary bodies became suddenly simple, even intuitive. That's what made his outlook so valuable and useful.

In a similar way, when we consider Christ in all the scriptures as backward-looking, we feel an emotive objection rise. Every fibre of our being wants to glorify Christ in His incarnation. The Cross is the centre of everything, right?

Well, it is . . . *for us.*

It marks the pivot point of our lives and the history of the world; it is the ultimate before and after moment.

But what if the cross isn't the centre of history?

What if we shift our point of view? Could it be that a new reference point might diffuse a whole lot of complexity in our understanding of the purposes of God— in scripture, and in our lives?

What happens when we place ourselves, scripture, and even Christ incarnate, in orbit around an original story, established before time began?

An explosion of simplicity!

With the backstory of God as our ultimate point of reference, life comes into sudden focus.

Enter the Hero and the villain, and the two scripts that retell their tale.

Jesus' life does not simply *define* heroism.

He perfects what it means to play the hero!

He was the author and perfecter of the hero script. He wrote the script before history began; He perfected it in His life, ministry, death and resurrection.

As the hero, like Muhammad Ali in the 1977 film, "The Greatest," he played himself in the role.

All His miraculous acts rely on a recognition of His association with the hero script. Mary sees it and His ministry begins. Demons catch on and they bow and submit. Peter proclaims it and his declaration of Christ's identity as the anointed Son forms an important pivot point in the incarnation story. "You are the Anointed One. You are the Son."

"Now that you have made the connection," says Jesus (my paraphrase), "we have something solid to build on. The rest of the story can unfold"

As for us, throughout history, we as humanity find ourselves playing the villain. All our pride, vitriol and self-serving behaviour is on display. Centuries of backstabbing and betrayal, bloodshed and broken hearts leave a horrible aftertaste.

We needed saving from ourselves, needed some way to get off the villain script. And so, in steps Jesus. To get the job done, He not only plays the Hero; He also takes the part of the villain. When it came time for us to face a frightening fall from grace, another stepped in to take our place.

Jesus embraced the role; robbed of all dignity and soundly rejected by all, He swapped parts with us. When things looked bad for us, like a veritable stunt double, Jesus took the fall. Redemption for us is possible because we have been picked up off the villain script and placed into the hero narrative. Jesus voluntarily sets us up to dispossess . . . Himself!

Heb 12:2 | John 2:5-11 | Mark 3:11 | Luke 4:41 | Matt 16:13-20

These two scripts form the basis of the spiritual mechanics behind the atonement, the great exchange and our undeserved place and position—found in the beloved, lavished upon by the Father, with all the rights and privileges we now experience in Christ.

"No one comes to the Father except by me."

"I am the way."

This is a deeper understanding behind what Christ achieved for us.

The villain's wages are the curse, disgrace. Ultimately, they are hung on a tree as a public example of the result of their poor choices. The curse and the tree are a package deal. Haman, Absalom and Jesus all die—hung up for all to see, all reaching a point where the only purpose they could yet serve was as a monument of shame and a warning to others.

To take the curse, Jesus played the part of Lucifer in his fall from grace.

Paul in Galatians says it like this, "He became a curse for us." In other words, He played the part of the villain, so we would not have to.

He took our place and set us free from the terrible fear of a wasted life.

Jesus threw away His life and potential. He ruined His life on purpose.

He wasted everything He could and should have been. He became what we most feared, what we deserved, to be—an example of the fruits of a life governed by foolish pride and bad choices.

2 Cor 5:21 | John 14:6 | Gal 3:13

Q1.   What does it add to your worship of Christ, when you join up the different aspects of our hero's story and identity?

Q2.   What difference does it make to you if "Christ in all the scriptures" references pre-history rather than the incarnational period in His story?

Q3.   When Jesus, beginning with Moses and the prophets, explained to the disciples on the road to Emmaus 'the things concerning Himself,' their hearts 'burned within them.' What is your heart response when you consider that Christ may have spent that journey explaining from scripture not His incarnation, but His eternal backstory?

Prayer.

Lord. Our hearts are full of Christ, and we feel a warmth within. We long to connect with the glory He had before the world was. We deeply desire for our worship to be unlocked. Unshackle it from space and time and any reference point imposed upon it, so we can stand close and behold the face of our God and saviour, and see Him for who He truly is. We want to know him. Make Your word burst with flavour and richness as we seek Him within its pages.   Amen.

CHAPTER SEVENTEEN

A CURSE FOR US

HE TOOK A RUNNING LEAP AND VOLUNTARILY PLUNGED HEADLONG DOWN THE SLIPPERY SLOPE AND INTO RUIN.

The dawn of the curse in Jesus' experience begins in the Garden of Gethsemane. As we creep closer in the darkness, we find Him in prayer, wrestling with His father, perhaps for the first time in His life. He is offered a cup He does not wish to drink.

In it is the curse in liquid form.

It was a poisoned chalice, and *ruined life* filled it to the brim.

No one in their right mind would have put it anywhere near their lips. Eventually, however, Christ agreed to His father's request; in the spirit, He raised the cup high and drank deeply of every drop.

The venom immediately went to work.

No sooner had He tasted its bitterness than the curse hit home—hard.

Immediately a dear friend betrayed Him into the hands of the authorities and He was arrested. Minutes later, its effect could be seen again when His other friends forsook Him and fled into the night. The curse cut deep into His relationships— He was despised and rejected, the normal symptoms of a ruined life after it has progressed a significant distance down the slippery slope.

Luke 22:39-23:46

Next, the leaders and authorities within His community turned against Him. In a hurriedly-put-together kangaroo court, lies and accusations against Him filled the air. It was as if whole world had turned in a moment.

Everything had gone to custard.

He had routinely walked in significant levels of favour, but now everyone was against him. All He had ever done for others—all the love and care and miracles, the help He had offered so many—became suddenly irrelevant.

In a moment, all His life's successes and achievements slipped away, His reputation quickly lost in a haze of accusation. Any opportunity to obtain justice fell from his grasp. The curse was unrelenting, intent only on his complete destruction. No one saw good in Him anymore.

Jesus was alone, forsaken, humiliated . . . and hope was fading fast.

He was used to receiving His share of flack in life. For the last three years He had been subjected to plenty of snide remarks. The odd hater who didn't like His message or thought one of his miracles was undeserved or badly timed had taken Him to task often enough. But this was different. So much of what represented authority and decency in His world now pointed a reproachful finger at Him. He could just about taste the tactile hate in the air around Him.

Silent most of the time, when He opened his mouth, He received a slap across the face for His trouble. From Caiaphas's trial to Herod's palace, allegations gave way to gloating and merciless mocking.

His rapid slide into despair continued as the curse left Him unheard, humiliated and alone.

Then pain arrives, approaching without hesitation only to grip Him like a vice. Knocked down and disorientated, He stands again, and the torment continues.

The hurt and injury escalate to excruciating levels.

Soldiers tear His back open with a lash. Pain and humiliation merge as a thorny crown is pressed onto His head.

A creeping realisation closes around Him until He is convinced all hope and help have become completely out of reach.

No one stands with Him.

No reprieve is in sight.

He tries to focus but can only vaguely keep his attention on Pilate and his political pandering as he plays games with His life. Jeers rise to a roar and Pilate's suggestion of a final reprieve for Him is drowned in a thunder of hate-filled voices.

Confusion and fear.

"This can't be real. This is not fair! What did I do to deserve this?"

Most who find themselves on a slide into despair and ruin take some time to descend. It might start with some slight rebellion or a petty theft. Then they fall in with bad company. Slowly good character is corrupted. Then increased exposure to violence causes hardness to take hold. Light drug use gives way to heavy addiction and more serious crime feeds the habit. Eventually, decent people no longer find it tolerable to be around them. In the end, the only other company they can find is of their own kind. Finally, their fall opens them to public ridicule; they are good for nothing other than as a lesson in the consequences of bad choices.

In less than twelve hours, Christ moved from a blessed and favoured life with the pleasures of long-standing friendships to a situation beyond understanding.

No one falls this far overnight, but . . .

Jesus literally plummeted from grace.

It was as if the curse in the cup was super-concentrated. He ran and took a fearless leap. He voluntarily plunged headlong down the slippery slope and into ruin.

Now He stumbles along, condemned to die, driven along the road. His wounds are severe and His strength is waning. He carries a wooden cross, too heavy by far—especially in his condition. The crowd murmurs as He passes. How could they make sense of His rapid fall from grace?

Soldiers strip Him naked and hurl Him down upon the wooden cross. Strong, rough arms hold Him down as nails are belted into his wrists and feet. Horror and trauma engulf His person.

Pain is everywhere.

His mind is overwhelmed, and it screams . . .

"No, no, no! This has gone too far! Why does no one stop them?"

In the fog of His agony He realises His vigilant angelic protectors are standing back. Now they watch from afar. His expectation of His own survival ebbs away until finally it disappears entirely.

He hears the grunts of effort as the guards raise the cross, then, with a tremendous jolt, His world spins and a whole other level of agony descends on him.

Crucifixion steals his breath and never gives it back—every gasp is agony.

Taunts and mocking.

He has become a spectacle for all. He hangs on a tree as a cosmic testament to the inevitable end of the cursed . . . his purpose in life diminished until He is only useful as an example of *what not to do with your life.* The only companions He has left are thieves. The only voice raised in His defence is a criminal's, hanging alongside Him on Rome's equivalent of Death Row.

Finally, Jesus voluntarily embraces death and in doing so, He arrives at the curse's final destination. He takes His last breath, alone, forsaken and humiliated. All His potential has come to nothing, His years cut short as He dies before His time. His life is shamefully wasted and ruined.

He became a curse, and in so doing,
traded His place with me, the villain.
He, the Hero, swapped our scripts,
took my disgrace, and chose instead,
to make a hero out of me!

Luke 23:26-46

No failure for me now. No wasted years, and no dead end alleys. No fear of getting it wrong. No ridicule, shame, or disgrace. No accusing pointing fingers. I am empowered to boldly reach for my destiny; I can take risks and make audacious moves forward. I can claim my inheritance though its road is fraught with obstacles, though opposition resolves to block my way, reject my claim, and hinder all my efforts.

One moment changed it all.

> When my Saviour drank the bitter cup, He took it from my hand.

> And placed His cup of blessing there instead.

1 Cor 10:16

Q1.   Compare this view of the great exchange (His righteousness for my sin) and the traditional analogy focussed on the balances of His and my ledger books? What does it mean for Christ? What does it mean for me?

Q2.   What has happened to the fear of failure for us if we walk in intimacy with the Lord?

Q3.   To procure our salvation, Christ needed to bind His story to that of the ultimate villain, Lucifer. It was like a swim in cement shoes. Have you ever seen the destructive power of the villain script in your life or the lives of those you love?

Prayer.

Lord. Who knew the horror, wretched shame and agony Christ would bear for us? We worship our precious saviour and determine not to waste His sacrifice, not to minimise His pain. We stand tall in the presence, irrespective of our doubts and inadequacies. We stand to honour him. We stand in belief. We choose to believe the promise of Your redemptive purpose for us. We trust You to hold us up and keep us from failure and disgrace. Keep the cross of Christ before our eyes and birth new hope in us.   Amen.

CHAPTER EIGHTEEN

PARRAMATTA GRIDLOCK

THEIR WORDS AND HANDS AND HEARTS VIBRANTLY
INTERTWINED, PRODUCING NEXT-LEVEL CREATIVITY
OUT OF DEEP INTIMACY.

I woke before first light. By the time I was packed and ready, Hussein my adopted taxi driver was already parked at the front of my house, ready to drive me to the airport. An hour later, I thanked him for the ride, boarded my flight and landed in Sydney at around eight a.m., just in time to hire a car and commute across town. My client that day was a large company in the Western Suburbs.

I only got as far as Parramatta when I found myself in a gridlock. Sitting behind the wheel, stuck at an intersection, I zoned out, and in a sort of daydream, wondered how long it would take for the traffic to clear.

In the boredom of the moment, a seemingly random idea dropped into my head.

"What if I went on a quest to search for Jesus in the creation story?"

"He was there, right?"

I wondered whether it was possible to create a red-letter version of creation, like one of those New Testaments where the words of Christ are highlighted in red.

I was enthralled!

It felt more like inspiration rather than deduction and so I made a mental note to investigate the idea after work when I got back to my apartment.

The traffic moved on and so did I.

It turned into a long day wrestling with technology.

I arrived back late and grabbed a quick takeaway dinner, and then my mind turned again to the revelation of the morning. With a pen and paper in hand I opened my Bible to the first chapter of Genesis.

"Hmm, let's see. The Father spoke and it was done. Christ, the Son, created everything as the work of His fingers. I'll divide it up, based on those two verses—words verses actions."

I was engrossed. I found myself gazing through a fresh window into the mystery of our world's first moments.

The Father asks for light—a word. Christ eagerly responds. He creates the light—an action. He revels in the wonder of it. In fact, He enjoys the newly-created light so much He purifies it, separating it from the darkness. Then He goes further still—He's caught up in the moment—and before we know it, He goes ahead and creates a whole mechanism whereby light and dark cycle back and forth to mark the passing of the days.

"Christ did so much more than He was asked!" I exclaimed to myself. "He responded with so much enthusiasm and positivity. Remarkable!"

The next day the Father picks up on what His son has done. Taking the idea of separation even further, He responds in delight. "Let there be a firmament!" He says, "a wide expanse of sky separating two bodies of water—the sea and the clouds—from one another."

Separation, differentiation, filling . . . suddenly I could see how all through the first chapter of Genesis the Father and the Son were feeding off each other's ideas, taking them further, winding each other up in a sense, until creation bursts forth in a ridiculous array of glory!

"Wow!" I thought to myself. "They were completely uninhibited! As the Father and the Son excitedly engaged with each other, it was like their words and hands and hearts vibrantly intertwined, producing next-level creativity out of deep intimacy."

Gen 1:3-5 | Gen 1:6-8

"What a privilege." I felt the awe of the moment.

It was getting late . . . but there was one more facet to explore.

My mind went to a verse of scripture:

> *I was right beside the LORD, helping him plan and build. I made him happy*
> *each day, and I was happy at his side.*

"What if that verse speaks of the Holy Spirit, not—as I'd always presumed— Jesus?"

This was a new insight. The third person of the Trinity was on stage now, and He was beautiful both in form and function.

I saw the Spirit as the architect and designer of it all, rejoicing in the moment, advising Jesus on the flavour of each of His responses to the Father . . .

"Wait!" I thought. "This is not just a conversation. It is something akin to a lovers' quarrel."

I was completely dumbfounded at what I heard in my spirit. It was a conversation between themselves, about themselves.

It went like this:

The Father says,

> "Let there be light."

The Holy Spirit, the architect, whispers in Christ ear,

> "Make it about the two of you. Make it art!"

So Christ makes the light, delighting in it, separating it from the darkness in a marvellous procession of coming together and moving apart again.

"Dunah! There you go!" He says to His father. "I'm making a picture of us! You are so bright and glorious compared to me! We are like light and darkness compared to each other. But when We are together, look what happens! It's My favourite part of what I've made, the setting of the day—the glorious colours that represent how We feel when We are together."

Prov 8:30 | Gen 1:3

The Father responds:

"Nice work, but you go too far. We are of the same substance. How about tomorrow you separate water from water, instead of light from dark?"

And so Christ goes to work, but He chooses to perform the task vertically rather than horizontally. In doing so, He declares . . .

"Yes, we are made of the same stuff; still, you are so much higher than I!"

"Okay, okay," declares the Father with a grin. "How about this? Let's make us on the same level, but you are more tactile than I, like land beside water . . ."

The tongue in cheek tussle continued . . . but I fell asleep.

Q1.   In creation, the Trinity seems lost in the moment. When have you experienced something like that?

Q2.   The three of them seem to use creation to creatively portray who they are in relationship. How do you submit to this romance of the Spirit in your life and relationships?

Q3.   If humanity is "made in His image," how could we align with this to live out our purpose as part of creation?

Prayer.

Lord. We act, work and create to achieve outcomes and accomplish purposes. You act to glorify yourself, to externalise the hidden wonder of your story and who You are. You bless those around You because of the incredible fullness of Your person. Bless us and make us a clear retelling of Your joy and story together so our life becomes a piece of creation in resonance with Your original intent.   Amen.

CHAPTER NINETEEN

WORTHY COMPANION

IT WAS LIKE THE INNOCENCE OF YOUTH, WITHOUT
ANY OF THE SELF-CONSCIOUSNESS ASSOCIATED
WITH ADULTHOOD.

The picture of the Father and Son in creation is alive with detail. The two figures are in community; it is a fruitful relationship out of which life springs forth. A sun and moon stand in the centre of a sky filled to bursting with stars. The sky and the seas teem with life. So does the land.

And on the land, a garden with two trees in the centre retell the same story.

The two trees express the character of those they represent. Christ, the source of life, stands beside the Father, the unapproachable source of all wisdom and knowledge. So too, the tree of life stands beside the tree of the knowledge of good and evil.

When Eve, therefore, was forbidden to approach or eat of one of those trees, it was not a random test whereby mankind was doomed to certain failure. That tree represented something sacred—a portrayal of the one who abides in light, who no one can look upon and live . . . the Father.

But let's go back a day or two. Father and son have finally decided. "It's time for our masterpiece. Let's make mankind in our image."

Making humanity in their image required a portrayal of them both, so they created a man and a woman, two standing together, a duo representing them as a self-portrait.

Gen 1:16, 20 | Gen 2:8-17 | Gen 1:26

Adam and Eve's place of rule and mandate to multiply completes a vivid portrayal of the Father and the Son. Just as the garden had two trees surrounded by many trees and the sun and moon was encircled by clusters of stars, so the first traditional family conveyed the glory of an interplay of creative genius—motivated by something a little like romantic love.

They say truth is stranger than fiction.

I never expected creation to be so light and playful.

Father and son appear distracted with joy in what they had become to one another—like the innocence of youth, without any of the self-consciousness associated with adulthood.

My heart leapt. I wanted some of what they had for *our* marriage, *our* life and family.

God comes to Adam and together they go through what, on the face of it, seems like a strange ritual. They are seeking a mate for Adam, examining one animal after another—without success.

None are suitable.

None are a good enough match.

Eventually when all options are exhausted and no suitable companion can be found, God takes one of Adam's ribs while he sleeps and makes Eve out of it.

When he wakes, it's problem solved. Man and woman have been made for each other and they find delight in companionship together.

God's artistic renditions have morphed from the rhythm of day and night, through many iterations, to now become animated flesh-and-blood models of themselves—two companions, lost in delight with each other.

In an uninterrupted flow, God is still telling His story. The animals in this drama are playing the part of the angels—amongst them, God could find no suitable companion.

Gen 1:26-31 | Gen 2:18-25

[Ezekiel's living creatures with heads of lion, ox and eagle existed prior to creation, pre-dating the animals made on day six to represent them—live extras brought in for the retelling. Eventually, after Lucifer's betrayal, and out of the ashes of defeat, God finds a companion from within *Himself*. And so the beauty of Trinity rises—the epitome of companionship, love, collaboration and unity. No one else, no created being would satisfy. Deity re-formed, from one into a fellowship of three, and joy finally arrived for them. This mystery is retold at the birth of our world, and the chosen genre is a pantomime.]

The hero script alone was woven into creation. All the imagery focusses on the Son—the Hero—and His relationship with the Father. The villain does not feature except for a transient reference to his inadequacy—no angel could truly satisfy the heart of a perfect God.

This was enough to irritate the king of all fallen fiends. It reminds him of his deficiencies and his fall. He was never enough, could never be enough. In his eyes, he had been set up to fail.

How dare they come here and rub it in.

For eons, 'darkness was upon the face of the deep'—only, the watery prison, once so appropriate to his mood, is now awash with life, light, colour and beauty. All of creation rings with one idea . . . God has finally found delight.

The joy and gladness of the moment diminished Lucifer as an eternal has-been, one who would not and could not measure up, one found inexorably wanting.

Jealousy and hate in dragonish form slither over to the newly formed couple with a malicious plan. He would immediately deface the creator's masterpiece and he would add to it a touch of Himself in the process.

Tempted, the couple overreached . . .

    . . . and they fell as Lucifer fell.

Death, sin and the curse arose to join the original intention of life, dominion and blessing. The law of sin and death took hold . . . to reign until the time when incarnation interrupted the perfect communion of the Father and His beloved son.

Ezek 1:10 | Gen 1:2 | Gen 3 | Rom 8:2 | Rom 5:12 | Matt 27:46

Q1.   How does the imagery of a lonely search in God's backstory help us understand His attitude toward us in the present day when we experience loneliness ourselves?

Q2.   How might it inform our view of the present day dynamics within the Trinity, His attitude to us as His children?

Q3.   Reflect on God and the enemy's attitude towards love, marriage and family. What is it about the backstory of God and their shared history that is behind their opposing views?

Prayer.

Lord. Your story leaves our theology tasteless and our emotions overwhelmed. We want to know and be known and to be caught up with the dance of Your sweet communion together. As You invite us in, we worship Your reality, vulnerability and authenticity. Yours is a perfect and sacred heart once disappointed and deeply wounded, now lavish and full toward us. We wanted an invulnerable God to keep us safe but You revealed yourself as one who loves without reserve or self-protection. You have drawn us and we lean in — to taste and see that You are truly good.   Amen.

CHAPTER TWENTY

THE LONELY SEARCH

HE WANTS US TO UNDERSTAND THAT
HIS BACKSTORY INCLUDES A DEGREE
OF LONELINESS AND LONGING.

What would you get if you took another Adam, a man perfect in strength, form and vigour, prior to the fall—and placed him in an everyday-life situation? He would struggle to fit in, right?

But what if you went further and placed him in a country long defeated—a nation dejected by enemy oppression? Not only would he not feel at home, he would be like a powder keg in a lightning storm! What would happen when his untarnished optimism and innocence encountered the depression and gloom of his nation and people?

You might think this experiment sounds like the result of a twisted mind. And yet, just such a scenario occurred. In fact, it was divinely inspired and motivated, not by a wicked sense of humour, but by a desire to retell an important personal story.

Samson is a portrait of a man born out of time and place. His incredible dominion over animals is a nod to the original mandate given to Adam and Eve. His strength and charisma did not play out well in the eyes of the enemy.

We are quick to criticize Samson's erratic love life, especially after it comes to a head with a disastrous liaison with a prostitute. But, although such behaviour is hardly good form for Christians, his life purpose remains intact—Samson remains a type of God in ages past; his life giving us an important parallel with the story and heart of God.

Judges 13-16

Think of the likeness! His quest for a bride is remarkable. He is larger than life, untouched physically, mentally or emotionally by the national defeat of his people. He reaches the age where boys show an interest in girls, and amongst his own people he finds potential mates undernourished, over-serious, and generally depressed and miserable company.

He is revolted.

There is nothing there for him.

When his father sends Samson on an errand into Philistine territory, to his surprise he sees the first girl to ever make his heart beat faster.

She is more like him.

Okay, she is not a tonne of solid muscle, but she is tall and sweet and, who knew, full of enthusiasm and mirth.

When he returns home, he says to his parents, "She is the one for me."

He soon finds out, however, that the forces of oppression reach even to his fiancé. The wedding is hardly over when she caves in to threats of violence against her family and divulges the answer to his riddle. She is as intimidated as the rest of them!

"Not her as well!"

It ends when she and her family are killed . . . by her own people, and Samson remains without a suitable companion. After twenty years as judge to Israel and after years of labouring to bring his nation into peace, he is still . . . alone.

Finally, he finds Delilah, a woman who remains unbowed even to the oppressor. She is free of every moral, political and social constraint.

"Could *she* be the one?"

Imagine his disappointment as he wakes. She too can be manipulated. What a waste of time! What a disappointment. He finds himself laid bare, rendered helpless by the betrayal of an intimate friend.

Judges 14:1-3 | Judges 14:12-15:6 | Judges 16:4

Could this incident be a retelling of the moment where God Himself fell prey to betrayal for greed and gain? Could these fickle caresses in the brothel somehow sacredly point to the ultimate and original infidelity?

We are so used to our view of a Teflon-coated God. When we hold stiffly to our doctrine of the Trinity's perfect joy, omniscience and omnipotence, it is difficult to think of God as ever caught up in the middle of a bad day. Yet, in the narrative He seems to want to communicate is that He has a backstory, one that includes a degree of loneliness and longing, suffering and regret.

What a surprising source of comfort this is to us, as we navigate the ebbs and flows of our ordinary lives.

Samson's story continues into calamity, distress and loss. There is hopelessness and defeat.

Glory was interrupted.

Could Samson's story be a demonstration of just how bad it got during the rebellion of Lucifer in heaven?

Why is it that cities and temples in the Bible fall down? Is it because the original city also once fell? Could all wars, in essence, retell the trauma of a primeval one? Perhaps one war in the eternal backstory has seeded and empowered all the horror associated with all the conflicts down through history!

In my mind, the Philistines brought Samson into their temple on his final day to mock him and then murder him. They were set on his complete humiliation. He was off script, as his captivity and helplessness so publicly demonstrated.

Still, in his last moments, God touched Samson in a subtle and glorious way. Perhaps half an hour before his life would have ended (if his enemies had their way), God gave him an idea, and then restored his strength so he could follow through with it. I see Samson moving to the mighty pillars, placing his hands on their cold, honed surface and pushing them apart. The temple falters, and then topples. Everyone inside perishes, including Samson.

Judges 16:18-21 | Judges 16:23-30 | 2 Chron 36:19 | Josh 6:20-21 | Josephus 7.1.1

A martyr's death beneath the rubble represented a dramatic shift that propelled Sampson's end from that of a villain—a man fallen from grace—to that of a victorious hero. It was touch and go how Samson's story would end; God's last-minute intervention, however, ensured that Samson would not die a failed leader, completely off-script, tortured, disgraced and defeated.

It cost him a few moments of his life, but the resulting destruction of the Philistines and their temple restored the glory of his life. In the nick of time, God had adjusted the narrative, bringing His man back on-script! If things had continued unabated, his story would have been one of disobedience followed by an irrecoverable demise—the villain's story. Instead, Father God aligns Samson's betrayal and demise within the ruins of a temple to a similar tragedy within His own story.

Lucifer reached for the throne of heaven, and in the war and carnage that followed, there seemed no end to the fallout and consequences of his raw and wicked ambition. Is Samson's last moment a window into the moment where the true king of heaven was first betrayed and then left for dead amongst the ruins of His once-glorious city and temple?

And Samson's experience is not unique. Could it be that Jeremiah and his famous lament amidst the ruins of his city alludes to the same picture?

God has a backstory that includes unimaginable pain, grief and loss.

What does that mean for us?

It frames our world.

It began in the Garden of Eden. Eating from the tree of life instantly bound us to the script and destiny of the Hero—the glorious Son of God. That was the plan for humanity.

But when we ate of the other tree, humanity was suddenly aligned with the Father's story. Now two possibilities opened up—good *and* evil. One bite opened us up to the blessings He had experienced alongside the Son . . . and the curse and consequence associated with His friendship with Lucifer.

Judges 16:28-31

To eat the forbidden fruit was to embrace the Father's narrative and taste the bittersweet possibilities which would resolve into two scripts, two pathways and two destinies.

Instead of the future and destiny of humanity carrying a singular promise of ceaseless blessing, the plight of people everywhere became an uncertain journey with blessing and curses both a possibility.

Would we play the part of the Hero or the villain?

I imagine myself there, hearing Samson's groan as he takes a last breath, bloody and beaten, with the dust and rubble and the ruins of the temple upon him. As I stand and wonder, I hear a quiet voice over my shoulder, a quiet murmur . . .

"If you eat of the other tree, you will surely die."

Gen 2:17

Q1.   Reflect on the book of Hosea, 1 Cor 13 and Samson's story as they speak to the challenges of exemplary but unrequited love?

Q2.   Consider this period before time began as it has been described so far. How bad did the betrayal and fall of Lucifer and the war in heaven get?

Q3.   The same power - If a divine near-death experience in the backstory of God empowered Christ's resurrection, what might Romans 6:10-11 and a life on-script mean to you?

Prayer.

Lord. Your pain is beautiful and glorious. We want to weep with You awhile, and meet You in the ruins as Your eyes ran down with tears. In betrayal, destruction, pain, loneliness or disappointment, help us to find in our grief a connection with You and Your story so we glory in our sufferings and grow in and through them. We ask You to intervene in our choices. Redeem the narrative of our lives, we pray.   Amen.

CHAPTER TWENTY-ONE

UNDER THE RUBBLE

THE FATHER'S HEART DOES NOT BREAK
FOR HIMSELF, BUT FOR THOSE WHO
HAVE BECOME HIS ENEMIES.

I imagine God's social media feed—full of selfies taken throughout His life, from eternal ages until creation's dawn.

"Hang on! No digital cameras or smart phones here! Only old-school technology is appropriate to capture images more archaic even than ancient history."

"So maybe a photo album rather than Instagram . . ?"

"Let's settle for an antiquated roll of film instead. Look over there!"

We settle on the couch and turn our eyes to a flickering image on the wall.

The projector whirrs.

Suddenly, there, on the screen, we see God. And He's all alone.

He precedes the whole created order. When we see Him, back there in the beginning of beginnings, He's all by Himself.

The film runs through the projector, frame by frame, for hundreds of rolls. It's just God up there, on the screen.

And then, something shifts and we catch a glimpse of His creative genius. He who is love personified, has started making creatures to love and care for.

First God makes a prototype, then, driven by excellence, He adapts His approach with each iteration. These creatures are something akin to the animal-like angels we read about in scripture, usually deep in the books of the prophets—like Ezekiel's army of living-creatures with four different types of heads or Daniel's horned creatures. They start out plain and simple, but before long they emerge, a medley of colour and character—angels of every shape and size!

Soon our screen is filled with an array of attendants more human in form, Zechariah's colour-coded guards of the four winds, Isaiah's six-winged bodyguards, Elijah and Elisha's fiery charioteers, and then there's archangels and heavenly choirs.

He is surrounded now! He's made a heavenly civilisation!

But something about the look on God's face tells us He's still not satisfied. He's going from one to the other, shaking His head. They're all magnificent, for sure, but none of them seem to be quite what he'd longed for . . . a fit companion.

On the one hand, God could make a being who is a little boring but will not be too much trouble—their conversation and company would not be satisfying in the long run. On the other hand, he could decide on a more challenging personality for his creation—a more equal match, that could eventually pay dividends in terms of enjoyment!

God seems to be warming to the second option, with each iteration.

His expression changes. It seems He's had an idea.

It's time to create His masterpiece.

Our eyes widen as this latest being emerges. This angel makes all the creatures around him seem only study pieces, or practice strokes.

Now God has someone beside him.

A seemingly fit companion.

Lucifer.

Ezek 1 | Dan 8 | Zech 6 | Isa 6 | 2 Kings 2:11 | 2 Kings 6:17 | 1 Thess 4:16
Jude 1:9 | Job 38:7 | Luke 2:13-14 | Gen 2:18-20 | Ezek 28:12

This highest angel of all takes his place as God's second-in-command and closest friend.

God's retinue was complete, yet with the joy of a pleasant companion comes the risk of a combative and prideful heart.

The delightful menagerie then turns and makes their way through the deep— the empty wastes of space and time. The Father has turned His heart towards ideas of home. At His word, a mountain forms out of the nothing, and they find their journey's end.

My make-believe film captures it all, as He and His creatures work as one to build a heavenly mountain home. Lucifer heads the work. Soon he will become mayor of a thriving metropolis.

All is as it should be. Civilisation grows. There is commerce and trade, festival and grandeur. It is as great as any empire in its heyday—a triumphant climax of culture and delight. There is beauty and joy, palaces and a temple, where the breath-taking worship of God emanates as the lifeblood of the realm. Glorious Zion, the city of God—His heavenly mountain home!

Then, from who knows where, the rot sets in. It starts in Lucifer's heart, and like a cancerous growth, it fills him . . . and spreads to some of his companions. Lesser angels join the rebellion until, with a critical mass established, civil war erupts in heaven. Immortals battle in horrible skirmishes. The noise of combat drowns out the music.

This intimate betrayal cuts horribly at the heart of God—a dagger driven deep while in a close embrace.

The splendid pinnacle of God's creation, now turned villain, has come to despise the worship of God—and the temple which is its centre. His envy peaks. His desire is to rid himself of the one adored by all, so he can take His place.

He would do it differently.

He would do it all his way. If only God and those confounded praise parties, worship medleys and trumpet blasts were gone for good.

Ezek 28

His plan is simple.

He will topple the temple with God and His most devoted followers inside. He will cut out the heart of heaven's culture and transplant himself as substitute into the bleeding void.

The film now crackles with snapshots of the fall of a glorious city, burning walls and rubble all around. The temple has collapsed, and God is left, covered in the heavy rubble that once was the structure of His place of worship. He finds His past glory overwhelmed by loss and grief.

The centre of it all is suddenly on the outer!

As it happens, His heart does not break for Himself, but for those He has long loved. They have turned their hearts from Him to become His enemies. He mourns the loss of Lucifer even while the friend-turned-fiend dances around and rejoices in His pain.

Q1.   He is the thief, the liar, the destroyer, the accuser. The attributes of Satan were concrete prior to creation. What is it like to live with someone on his script?

Q2.   How do the scripts and the backstory of God inform your response when negative events happen?

Q3.   Faced with rebellion, loss and destruction, in times past God began to "work all things for good." Reflect on His backstory and His propensity to do restorative and redemptive work. What does this mean in your life?

Prayer.

Lord. We enter Your gates with thanksgiving and Your courts with praise. We come to Zion, the city of the great king and ponder all that is out of step with Your divine will. We stand beside You in Your passion to rebuild Your house and the heart of worship. Thank you. You have chosen us as Your dwelling place — a temple of God Most High. Yet You find us broken and bound. You find in us a ruin in want of repair. By Your grace build us up and make us glorious. Make of us a fit habitation for Your presence.   Amen.

CHAPTER TWENTY-TWO

THREE DIMENSIONS

MY BELOVED CHILDREN PLAYED THEIR PART
SO WELL. WHAT AN HONOUR TO WATCH ON
TO EACH TRIBUTE PERFORMANCE.

God seems unimpressed by my film and camera analogy. He wants to do one better! As we change the movie reel, He interjects.

"Let's take this up a notch. We need a dramatic performance with actors and characters on stage. We need sounds and smells and breath-taking sets to truly convey a sense of My past."

He snaps His fingers and we tumble through space and time to stand beside a shepherd boy as he sings his heart out, seated at the base of a tree, with a flock of contented sheep around him.

"It began like this," He says with a reminiscent air in His voice.

Before we know it, the scene has shifted and now the same boy is fighting a lion.

"Now look," He says, "The same scene from My life with a different actor and set."

The picture changes again and we see now a muscular young man attacked by a similar lion, his muscles bulging as he wrestles it to the ground until it breathes its last.

"One of My most dramatic experiments. The whole thing got a little out of hand," He chuckles.

1 Sam 17:34 | Judges 14:5-6

"My wonderful family grew and we prospered together," He mumbled contentedly to Himself,

We see a lone man wandering in a foreign land. Then the scene jumps forward in time. We see him set up a cluster of tents for his family. Next, he is surrounded by a swelling company, wealthy with stock and flocks.

The scene changes again.

We find ourselves presented with a charismatic leader of a ragamuffin band, in exile in the rocky wastes. They gather round him and hang on his every word.

"Those were great days," He exclaimed. "I remember that time with such joy! But I'm afraid there is sorrow coming up."

For a moment, we glimpse a giant of a man, innocently asleep, while a woman, obviously his lover, negotiates his price with a group of evil looking soldiers. We see the greed in her eye as she counts the coins she has been given.

At the edge of a forest, we hear a cry of desolation, uncontrolled and heart-breaking. It's the sound of an exiled king, overcome in his grief at the loss of a beloved son.

With emotions fatigued by one forlorn display after another, we continue to slip from scene to scene.

Another jump. We stand beside a man in ashes and covered in boils mourning the loss of beloved children and all his possessions.

For an instant, we stand beside a pillar to see a strongman give one last final heave, and we wince as the ceiling falls in our direction. Our last glimpse of his determined eyes will remain long, but thankfully, we do not. As the roof of the temple falls toward us, the scene disappears, to be replaced with another.

We stand at a distance to see a messenger share news with an old overweight man. We hear his cry of distress as he falls backwards to literally die of grief.

A city in ruins is the next stop on our quest to know our Lord. An old prophet weeps by the devastated walls. We listen to the dirge He sings over the

Gen 12-13 | 1 Sam 22:2 | Judges 16:19 | 2 Sam 18:33 | Job 2:8 | Judges 16:30

destruction and realise our companion and guide has been both poet and composer, a joyful tenor and a sorrowful bass.

A bald and plump, obviously wealthy Egyptian man screams in torment and pain at the realisation—his love will not and cannot be requited.

Now we ride on horseback quietly alongside a man dressed as an official of some ancient court. He is inspecting city walls, absolutely in ruins. We see his determined resolve to restore order are clear to all of us as we watch and we feel privileged to share in his melancholy vigil in the darkness.

In an instant, we move again, to stand atop a mountain beside a heavily whiskered wild-looking man. Devilish pagans dance around as if half-stupefied, evil is everywhere. The man looks up and shouts, "Enough!" and falls to his knees before a drenched sacrifice. Fire is flung downward from heaven in a mighty rush. We step back in alarm, amid a crazed chorus of defeat-ridden cries of anguish, and the scene fades and changes yet again.

Eventually, we return . . .

"It was My darkest hour. Each of My beloved children played their part so well. What an honour to watch each tribute to My life in theirs."

We have loitered long, and thus informed, we are full of questions but enlarged in our sense of His tragic history. When finally we set our foot on solid earth, in our own time and place, any doubts we have nursed concerning the heart of God have been silenced forever.

1 Sam 4:18 | Neh 2:12-15 | 1 Kings 18

Q1.   If the association of the scripts with the life of Samson and Eli and Potiphar somehow redeems their stories in our mind, what does it mean for you and your life?

Q2.   Have you ever sat in ashes or ruins, or experienced your live fall down around you?

Q3.   Have you ever been surrounded by evil and darkness as Elijah was and seen the fire fall?

Prayer.

Lord. We reflect on what You have suffered and still ourselves in wonder. Who knew You could suffer and be overwhelmed with pain and loss? You are the joy that seeks us through pain and what You have gone through opens our hearts and overcomes our petty grievances against an imagined God who knows little of what we have experienced. We determine that in our weakest hours we will run to you, the one who first experienced strength made perfect in weakness.   Amen.

HERO WORSHIP

He has delivered us from the power of darkness and conveyed us into the kingdom of the Son of His love, in whom we have redemption through His blood, the forgiveness of sins.

He is the image of the invisible God, the firstborn over all creation. For by Him all things were created that are in heaven and that are on earth, visible and invisible, whether thrones or dominions or principalities or powers. All things were created through Him and for Him. And He is before all things, and in Him all things consist. And He is the head of the body, the church, who is the beginning, the firstborn from the dead, that in all things He may have the pre-eminence.

For it pleased the Father that in Him all the fullness should dwell, and by Him to reconcile all things to Himself, by Him, whether things on earth or things in heaven, having made peace through the blood of His cross.

Colossians 1:13-20

Jesus Praying in the Garden

So far, we have reached for a new way of comprehending God—via His backstory. Our circumstances and indeed our world are all wired to retell this ancient and long-forgotten tale. We're intrigued, but we want to know more of this vitally significant tale of heroism and villainy . . .

Mostly, we want to understand more about *this hero*. Like the apostle Paul, we long . . . to know Him more.

So let's lean in, settle into our seats and ask the Hero to share His own story.

We already know Him as Saviour and Lord, but never before have we seen Him like this.

Come with me now, far back into the distant past and let the characters in scripture retell His tale. Let's catch a glimpse, from their lives, of the truly historic moment when . . . a hero arises!

PART
3

A HERO ARISES

HERO WORSHIP

He was oppressed and He was afflicted, Yet He opened not His mouth;

He was led as a lamb to the slaughter, And as a sheep before its shearers is silent, So He opened not His mouth.

He was taken from prison and from judgment, And who will declare His generation? For He was cut off from the land of the living; For the transgressions of My people He was stricken.

And they made His grave with the wicked—But with the rich at His death, Because He had done no violence, Nor was any deceit in His mouth.

Yet it pleased the Lord to bruise Him; He has put Him to grief.

When You make His soul an offering for sin, He shall see His seed, He shall prolong His days, And the pleasure of the Lord shall prosper in His hand.

He shall see the labor of His soul, and be satisfied. By His knowledge My righteous Servant shall justify many, For He shall bear their iniquities.

Therefore I will divide Him a portion with the great, And He shall divide the spoil with the strong, Because He poured out His soul unto death, And He was numbered with the transgressors, And He bore the sin of many, And made intercession for the transgressors.

Isaiah 53:7-12

Joseph sold by his Brothers

CHAPTER TWENTY-THREE

ANOINTING

WHEN THE VILLAIN STRIKES OUT AGAINST
THE FATHER, THE HERO IS THERE, AND HIS
ARRIVAL TURNS THE TIDE.

It's a cat and mouse game Saul and David are playing, an on-again, off-again friendship which eventually disintegrates into enmity and animosity. Saul starts off well. He is tall, handsome and strong, and when Samuel anoints him, the Spirit of God comes dramatically upon him. Victory follows him everywhere he goes. Saul is prospered and his fledgling kingdom is established.

But something is amiss; although it's hard to pinpoint the real issue, we are left with some unresolved questions. Why, for example, did Saul hide away amongst the baggage on his coronation day?

Of course, Israel had never had a king before, so to be their monarch was no doubt more than a challenge. Even so, Saul's response feels a bit off. If he's that anointed, why the need to hide? What's he really cowering from?

It seems from the very beginning, he knows he doesn't have what it takes. He knows his own inadequacy. And by the end, we all know it too. Saul's confidence-deficit opened a door to fear in his life—and it festers quickly. He soon becomes irrational. Something is not right in Saul's mind and heart. Inadequacy has given birth to jealousy. David's popularity, strength and glory is evident to all. He is a hero in the making.

"Saul has slain his thousands, and David his tens of thousands," he hears the people sing, and with that, Saul finally snaps.

1 Sam 10:22 | 1 Sam 18

Saul can no longer function in his role. He is tormented by evil spirits. Finally, deep-seated fear, rebellion and disobedience control him completely. When he resorts to dabbling in the occult, he further renders himself unfit for the office God had gifted him.

Just as he always feared, Samuel—and God—moves on to another man, anointing David in his place.

Nevertheless, Saul's place and position were irrevocable; he remained king until his death, but only as an impotent figurehead.

Understandably, David's road to the throne was uncomfortable and fraught; he was effectively an outlaw surrounded by ruffians and outcasts. Every victory made his relationship with Saul worse rather than better.

Saul and David are replaying the relationship dynamics between the original Hero and the villain.

Lucifer started well too, but like Saul, a deficit in his character eroded his ability to rule and function.

The Son would later rise to the throne of heaven, but in the meantime, He waits in Lucifer's shadow, just as David did with King Saul.

Christ, the Son didn't just have difficulties with Lucifer, the power of the day. He also had trouble closer to home.

In his early years, David was different from his brothers, and they spurned him—once when he brought them food on the battlefield and was caught up in the excitement of the moment, and another time, just before that, when Samuel came to their house to anoint a substitute monarch. He was the only brother excluded from meeting Samuel, left in the fields keeping the sheep.

Similarly, Christ, the Hero, was not like the others in heaven. He was divinity, something else entirely! Whatever He touched became glorious. And His every action was met with irritation and envy, especially on account of His relationship with His father.

1 Sam 18:7 | 1 Sam 15:10-35 | 1 Sam 28 | 1 Sam 16 | 1 Sam 22-31 | 1 Sam 16-17

That scene is seen most clearly in the life of Joseph—the gift of a marvellous coat of many colours was closely followed by mocking, rejection and murderous intent. Soon he was thrown into a pit and sold into slavery by his brothers.

His life articulates a parallel plot line, portraying a single truth—that the original Hero didn't fit in very well in the heavenlies, so long ago.

The Hero and the villain were drawn into rivalry and animosity.

And at some point Lucifer takes two new names—the Accuser and the Liar—as he falsely accuses the Hero.

Joseph can help us again with this part of the story. Potiphar plays the part of Father God and Potiphar's wife is the villain, who tries to turn the Hero toward the darkness. When he will not compromise her serpentine heart plots a betrayal as revenge. In a rapid turn of events, Joseph is accused and cast out of Potiphar's presence . . . into darkness.

Suddenly, Joseph and Potiphar are forced apart by a falsehood. Similarly, cunning rivals divide Daniel and the his king. They play him like a pawn against Daniel, using his own authority against his friend.

The Hero's trail turns downward into exile, humiliation and difficulty but He remains faithful and diligent.

Along the same lines, David flees as a criminal of the state into the wilderness. Daniel too is falsely accused. So is Jesus. So is Joseph. For all of them, things get worse before they get better. . . pits in the desert, lion's dens, prisons, caves in the wilderness.

Still, Joseph prospers despite the false accusation, and eventually we see him reinstated at an even higher level. David too, rises above. Daniel miraculously gets through a dark and fearful night in the lion's den.

When Pharaoh finds himself in need of insight, wisdom and someone able to manage the challenges of the day, Joseph is exalted. Within an instant, he is second only to the Emperor. And from there he begins to turn around the fortunes of kingdom and nation.

Gen 37 | Gen 39 | Dan 6 | 1 Sam 21:10 | Mark 14: 56 | Gen 41:41-45

Eventually, there is vindication, glory, adequacy and restoration.

No brief overview can adequately portray the long road between when David was anointed and when he finally received the crown. Lucifer was a fiendish adversary, slippery as a snake, and his reign lasted long. It probably seemed an eternity.

Saul hangs on to the throne, as does the original villain, Lucifer. That is until treason takes hold of him so that he rebels outright and strikes out against the Father. The Hero is there, and His arrival turns the tide but the kingdom is fractured by civil war.

Eventually, however, peace is restored. The Devil is at last cast down—his pride has become his undoing. The Hero stands in His place in glory at last!

In our parallel narratives, Joseph's relationship with his brothers is finally restored as he reigns alongside Pharaoh, and David eventually rules over a united kingdom. But the road to vindication has been long.

Gen 41:33-57 | 1 Sam 16:13-2 Sam 8:15 | Rev 12:7-9 | Ezek 28:17 | Gen 42-45

Q1.   Find yourself in the tale of Joseph. Identify yourself and anyone else you can think of in the narrative. Consider the scenes—For you, is it the time of dreams in a fancy coat, the rejection of the pit, faithfulness in Potiphar's house and the prison or the glory of the palace? How does this orientate you for the moment you are in?

Q2.   Now do the same with David's life as a template.

Q3.   With those two lives as your guide, find yourself as a character in the original story. The Father and the Son divided by Lucifer's lies and deception, times of Christ's humility and rejection and final vindication al before time and history began.

Prayer.

Lord, our heart is full of Christ. We have found a new reference point in him, yet grace us, because villainy is also alive and well in our souls . . . there are lies and deception in us. In fact, we confess the times we have taken advantage of power and position. You know how often our hearts rise in pride. We repent, to forsake wickedness and evil darkness when it seems to overwhelm. We choose to be heroic and embrace patience, faithfulness and humility.   Amen.

CHAPTER TWENTY-FOUR

GLORY INTERUPPTED

IT WAS A DEVASTATING ATTACK. THE
FATHER WAS VULNERABLE BECAUSE OF
THE INTIMACY OF THE RELATIONSHIP.

Earlier, we caught a glimpse of David and his son, Absalom. Let's turn to David as a point of focus. We want to linger for a moment on his story in the latter part of his life, as a picture of God our Father. We want to get to know *Him*—and David's life after he became king is instructive for us in this.

David reigned in Jerusalem, a city bustling with life, activity and festivity. Our Heavenly Father similarly reigned in Zion, the heavenly Jerusalem of which the earthly city was merely a copy, a picture. With Lucifer standing close, together they administered a wonderful cacophony of sights, sounds and glorious joy.

David was a charismatic ruler and the people loved him. His son Absalom was similar. The people loved him too. Then, Absalom turned on his father.

First, he spread lies to build a following for himself . . .

"David's deputies are much too busy to help you, but I have time for you."

Finally, he rebelled further, seizing power and forcing David to flee for his life. Yet, even in the ensuing struggle and exile , David is conflicted. His bond with Absalom and love for him does not waver. When he hears of his son's death, he grieves so bitterly, so deeply, that he earns a rebuke from his commander.

We are so used to a view of God in terms of absolute power, as though nothing could ever ruffle a hair on His head, but there was something about Lucifer's

1 Sam 5 | Heb 12:22 | Heb 8:5 | Col 2:16-17 | 2 Sam 15:3 | 2 Sam 18-19

attack that devastated Almighty God. Father God was vulnerable because of the intimacy of the relationship. Just as adultery cuts most deeply in the context of intimate love, this betrayal of a close friend hurt the heart of God—yet the Father stays His hand.

We see the same tussle in the heart of God demonstrated with rich clarity in the life of Hosea. Like Hosea, God was the faithful lover of an adulterous wife. His love is unrequited. Along similar lines, in Malachi, He is the father of a rebellious son. Again, Israel is playing the villain . . .

When Malachai reflects on this, he portrays God as saying,

"I have played My part more than adequately. Where is the honour due to Me?"

Father God, bound with the very one who attacked him, grieves but does not act against the villain even when there is plenty of justification for striking back or lashing out in retribution and judgement.

He is Love.

What does Love do in the face of betrayal?

Love is patient. Love is kind. Love is not easily provoked, and keeps no record of wrongs.

Listen to the heart-wrenching sobs for one who has wounded him so deeply! Hear David's grief over the death of his son. Here we have a window into the very heart of God when His once dear friend, now His betrayer, at last fell.

Reflect with me on just how profound David's grief was. We might call it 'over the top.' In fact his army commander's assessment of the situation was that David's grief posed a threat to the morale of the troops—to the point where he felt compelled to come right out and say so.

There is something fresh here for us to understand about Father God. It is amazing He is so motivated to retell this story. Who would have guessed His grief could so overwhelm Him?

Hosea 1-34 | Malachi 1:6 | 1 John 4:7-8 | 1 Cor 13 | 2 Sam 18

Perfect love seems too costly, but I find that reading this makes me love my Father more.

> *Then the king was deeply moved, and went up to the chamber over the gate, and wept. And as he went, he said thus: "O my son Absalom— my son, my son Absalom—if only I had died in your place! O Absalom my son, my son!"*

> *And Joab was told, "Behold, the king is weeping and mourning for Absalom." So the victory that day was turned into mourning for all the people. For the people heard it said that day, "The king is grieved for his son." And the people stole back into the city that day, as people who are ashamed steal away when they flee in battle. But the king covered his face, and the king cried out with a loud voice, "O my son Absalom! O Absalom, my son, my son!"*

> *Then Joab came into the house to the king, and said, "Today you have disgraced all your servants who today have saved your life, the lives of your sons and daughters, the lives of your wives and the lives of your concubines, in that you love your enemies and hate your friends. For you have declared today that you regard neither princes nor servants; for today I perceive that if Absalom had lived and all of us had died today, then it would have pleased you well. Now therefore, arise, go out and speak comfort to your servants. For I swear by the Lord, if you do not go out, not one will stay with you this night. And that will be worse for you than all the evil that has befallen you from your youth until now." Then the king arose and sat in the gate. And they told all the people, saying, "There is the king, sitting in the gate." So all the people came before the king. For everyone of Israel had fled to his tent.*

Absalom is dead.

Eventually David will reoccupy his kingdom and reign in Jerusalem once more. Eventually, another son, Solomon, will takes Absalom's place and position.

But for now, He mourns deeply.

2 Sam 18:33-19:8

This is sacred ground. The eternal God has bared His soul through David's fatherly grief and vulnerably shared His deepest secrets. It is a deep shock theologically to consider God the Father as conflicted or overwhelmed, but as we read scripture in this way, we find He is full of emotion—he feels, He patiently longs for His children to repent. He desires to protect them from the consequences of their actions, to journey with them through all sorts of peril— peril they have brought upon their own heads.

His generous-spiritedness and covenant faithfulness open him up all sorts of exploitation. This fact could make us feel a little unsafe. However, if Lucifer, the great villain himself could be mourned over like this, perhaps we should think again.

Maybe we are safer than we ever realised.

His power, eternity and faithfulness meld together, allowing Him to patiently take the long view. He holds out for those He calls His own to turn back to Him. In the end, He remains, His word remains, His kingdom remains, and all who have opposed Him are no longer in the scene or on the stage.

Besides Him now, is one perfectly superior and pure of heart—one who is gentle and humble of heart, able to justly rule from the throne of heaven and earth. Only the Son can be perfectly trusted with the cosmic equivalent of the nuclear launch codes.

Matt 11:29 | Phil 2:9 | Dan 7:13-14 | 1 Cor 15:20-28

Q1.   The kindness and patience of Father God leads us to repentance. What have you experienced of His generosity of spirit in your own life, when you have been out of step of His desires for you?

Q2.   What about your story, either your past actions or those of others, caused Father God to weep? Try a comparison with Absalom on for size, and reflect.

Q3.   How does the expansive father heart of God speak to your past regrets?

Prayer.

Lord, our hearts are villainous when compared to the measure of love and grace You offer us. We have seen much of Your kindness and desire it in its fullness but we pause at the threshold, timid at the thought that we might be another cause of sorrow for you. We seek You with care. We know Your tender love is sacred and Your companionship a deep privilege. Shoes in hand and with gentle tread, we step in Your direction to find a different kind of fear of the Lord. It rises within . . . a fear that we might presumptuously trample on delicate divinity.   Amen.

CHAPTER TWENTY-FIVE

THE POWER OF SONSHIP

WITHOUT DAVID, YOU DO NOT ATTAIN THE
GLORY OF SOLOMON BECAUSE THE ONE STOOD
ON THE SHOULDERS OF THE OTHER.

Lots of bad stuff flows down the generations. There is actually a name for this—iniquity. The same is true for the good. When Moses gives the law, he releases a revelation—that righteousness is generationally transmittable for a thousand generations. In like manner, wickedness too carries forward, though mercifully, it seems to become less potent over time.

> You shall not bow down to them nor serve them. For I, the Lord your God,
> am a jealous God, visiting the iniquity of the fathers upon the children to
> the third and fourth generations of those who hate Me, but showing mercy
> to thousands, to those who love Me and keep My commandments.

But as Jeremiah predicted, things change as we move into the new covenant. The cross contains intrinsic power that, when applied, can break longstanding chains and heal deep-seated wounds. There's no reason to live under the unfortunate legacy of past generations.

> In those days they shall say no more: 'The fathers have eaten sour
> grapes, And the children's teeth are set on edge.' But every one shall die
> for his own iniquity; every man who eats the sour grapes, his teeth shall
> be set on edge.

Ex 20:5-6 | Jer 31:29-30

Still, even in the New Testament, a purposeful alignment of our lives with the righteousness of our mothers and fathers is an essential prerequisite to receiving the blessings they hold.

This is how Paul puts it for us today:

> *Children, obey your parents in the Lord, for this is right. "Honor your father and mother," which is the first commandment with promise: "that it may be well with you and you may live long on the earth." And you, fathers, do not provoke your children to wrath, but bring them up in the training and admonition of the Lord.*

Good things happen when our children honour their parents. Honour is the key that unlocks the blessings, making them accessible for daughters and sons. The response of our children to us is crucial for them to receive what is theirs by right. That's the power of sonship.

Children, obey and honour. Parents, don't frustrate.

There are two sides to this coin if blessing is to be released, undiluted, from one generation to the next.

We've traditionally focussed on the need for children to obey. But there's a responsibility on the parent's too to make it as easy as possible.

We can either be parents that demand much of our children, or we can give them an unfair advantage by doing all we can to help them meet our expectations. Who would have thought that by lowering the bar, we can actually smooth the path for their feet and sure up their spiritual inheritance!

What if an absolute measure of our children's behaviour is less important than their posture toward their parents?

Everyone agrees that the next generation should thrive. We want things to go well for them. As parents, generous affirmation may be even more important in safeguarding the future of our family line, than any attempt by our children to live up to and behave in line with overly stringent behavioural expectations?

My personal take on this scripture is that it may be advantageous to ensure the bar is not too high for our children—hence the injunction to not frustrate or

Eph 6:1-4

exasperate our kids. It is an exercise in futility if we frustrate them in their attempt to connect with the blessing we carry.

In other words, what happens if we, as fathers and mothers, purposefully become less prescriptive about behaviour and more generous with our praise?

Yes. Idiot choices are irritating and they promise a bad end, but blessing is more significant a force than even the natural pull of cause and effect in this world. Blessing literally reverses the curse.

It seems that if we change how we engage with our children, we can realign the script for our sons and daughters!

What happened when Isaac was tricked into blessing a child that he had always, for cultural reasons, treated as *less than*?

That's right! When he inadvertently blessed his younger son, Jacob was indeed heartily blessed!

Amazingly, we are in a position, like Jacob, where we can cross our hands as we stand to bless. We are granted authority to bind and loose. We are the ones who are the destiny-shapers, and when we decide as parents to dote on our sons and daughters, always believing the best of them even in the context of accusation, the darkness is rendered impotent in their lives.

And so we take our cue from a father who ran down the road to embrace a rebellious son, lavishing him with treatment that seems unreasonable given he had squandered half the estate in wild living.

Are we prepared to cast our daughters and sons in the part of the Hero in their life script?

Or, will we believe the torrent of accusation, judge them, and push them away?

We are in the driver's seat, more than we ever realised. Imagine what would happen if we all let go of fear and judgement and refused to be played against our precious children?

Gen 27 | **Gen 48** | **Luke 15:11-23**

We know that the enemy loves to set us up to fail, then point the finger and try to shame us as publicly as possible. He is no different with our kids. He does the same toward them! Only, what he really wants, is for you to partner with him in shaming the very ones you love most of all.

We need to wake up to the fact that he is goading us. We must tame our natural inclinations until we are like the Father and our children are blameless in our sight.

Why?

Because the enemy's power as an Accuser rests on our agreement.

He fears, because he knows . . .

> that sonship is a dynamic that carries special promise,

>> that all his schemes evaporate when we reach out our hands to bless,

>>> and that he has no answer to a son or daughter with the correct stage and backdrop behind them, in costume and in character as the hero of the tale.

He has never had an answer to the power of the hero script!

So, we as parents can choose to align our families with the hero script. We can do the hard yards. We can face the difficulty of empty and humble times . . . and then set our kids up for a lifetime of the opposite—allowing them to continue our own well-established story.

There comes a significant moment where we must voluntarily step down.

We gesture to our rising children. At the right time, we step aside and allow an understudy to play the lead.

We're giving them permission to stand on our shoulders!

> Our ceiling will become their floor.

Eph 5:1 | Eph 1:4 | James 4:7, 11

Let's look at the power of this in action. For David, there was hardship, betrayal and exile; for Solomon there was only glory. Without David, the nation would never have attained the glory of Solomon's reign—the son stood on the shoulders of his father, the king who had gone before him.

Elijah knew loneliness and the intimidation of Carmel; Elisha, his spiritual son, received a double portion of his anointing and none of his sorrow. Likewise, the disciples did not experience the pain and anguish of Calvary, yet they inherited the authority Christ carried.

They all went further and climbed higher.

Here is the challenge. If we can suffer loss without bitterness, if we resist the temptation to question the character of God in our generation, we can bequeath a wonderful inheritance to the next!

We can say,

"Son, I led the way in the script, now you get to take it from here. Precious daughter, embrace the rest of the script. Take it from where I leave off, and soar. Go now from glory to glory!"

Genetically, we pass on what we have to give to our children at the moment of conception but our physical estate gets passed on when we die. Similarly, in the case of spiritual inheritance, it is the level we attain at the end of our lives that counts.

We are encouraged as we see Abraham, an old man stumbling up Mt Moriah, mustering his courage to pass one more faith test. Even when he has little left to give, he continues to enrich the inheritance Isaac and the nation of Israel would receive.

He passes the test, and then God speaks, "Now I can bless you."

And with that, the future of God's people is assured. In effect, God is saying:

"This measure of blessing is enough to carry your descendants through their time in Egyptian captivity, across the wilderness, and into the Promised Land. Your task is complete. *Now* the blessing you pass on will be sufficient for the generations to come!"

2 Sam 15-18 | 1 Kings 1-10 | 1 Kings 18:15-39 | 1 Kings 17-2 Kings 13 | Luke 23:33
John 14:12-14 | 2 Cor 3:18 | Gen 22:16

Q1.   Who are the father or mother figures in your life? Do you feel your connection allows you to stand on their shoulders?

Q2.   Who looks up to you in this way? How will you bequeath blessing to them?

Q3.   How have your desires to live in blessing been frustrated by others?

Prayer.

Lord, You are the one from which all other fathers take their name, the epitome and reference point for us all. Grace us to parent as You do, with lavish blessing, a generous spirit and wide-open arms for our children. Show us Your father-heart and fill our heart and hands so we have more than enough to pass on down the line to those who follow. We welcome You to father us in ways and to degrees we have never experienced before—speak and release Your lavish blessings over us.   Amen.

CHAPTER TWENTY-SIX

THE LONG GOODBYE

THE FATHER SEES IN THE SON ALL THAT
DELIGHTS HIS HEART, AND HAS ONLY
DISDAIN FOR LUCIFER'S FAILURE.

When Jacob woke to find he was not married to Rachel after all, but to Leah, her sister, he must have been enraged. All those years of work, only to be tricked once again! It would be seven more years before the situation was resolved.

Now he had two wives—one possessed a delightful x-factor, with the other, he had no chemistry at all. They were like chalk and cheese. What's more, throughout their life, contention existed between the two sisters as they vied for Jacob's affection.

A similar snapshot exists—think of the instant when Michal looks in disdain upon David as he dances wildly in ecstatic worship. We hear her criticism and wonder. *Does she know him at all?* Her true character is revealed in that moment, and it is out of step with David's own. She does not share the same heart, and quickly their intimacy fizzles. A few pages further along in the scripture, we find another woman in David's life, only she is entirely different. Abigail, in complete contrast to Michal, schools David in his own heart. Her industry and self-sacrifice to join him in exile aid his cause. She diminishes Michal by comparison.

All these stories provide subtle pictures of the Father. In each instance, He is found alongside a true companion and one that is deficient. They are all shadows of a story from long ago. Eventually, the Father sees in the Son all that delights His heart, and holds only distain for Lucifer's failure as a friend and confidant.

Gen 29:25-30 | Gen 30 | 2 Sam 6:14-23 | 1 Sam 25

The pattern is repeated in the life of Abraham, his legitimate wife Sarah and his relationship to his concubine, Hagar. One is a slave; the other is lawful, rightful, and free.

Elkanah also had two wives who lived in conflict with each other. Peninnah was so hard on Hannah. She was a bully, and it drove her to distraction. The world Elkanah lived in had disintegrated into violence and chaos—and so had his home life.

This was the past situation in heaven between the Father, the Son and Lucifer.

It's as messy a situation as any fictional love triangle.

Samuel, David and Saul give the most vivid and detailed portrayal of this, including the dynamics of how this tension eventually resolved.

Saul harasses David and makes his life difficult. But David prevails. Favour and victory follow him. Saul plays the part of the villain to a tee with his fiery temper and malicious jealousy.

Meanwhile, David in the role of the Hero, shows his submission to God. He refuses to arise against the Lord's anointed even when opportunities present themselves.

Eventually Saul goes too far. He crosses a line and then there is a substantive change. His crown will pass to David. In the meantime, Saul reigns as a lame duck. Slowly, by degrees David dispossesses Saul.

David becomes what Saul could never be. He carries himself so well, winning victory after victory. Soon the people sing his praises, and comparisons to Saul only serve to deprecate the king further.

Saul withers.

Darkness takes him.

He is filled with rebellion and fear until he can barely function. To think that heaven was once governed by one who fit the same description.

Throughout this entire saga, I feel the grief and disappointment of God.

Gal 4:22-23 | Gen 16:1-4 | 1 Sam 1 | 1 Sam 19 | 1 Sam 26:9 | 1 Sam 15-18

Worse still, it seems that an immutable word of God had sealed Lucifer's anointing, safeguarding his authority, position and place. This meant that both father and son could not act in the interim without loss of integrity. Their hands were tied. Even in the face of betrayal, they were unable to be anything other than faithful and true.

When I think of Saul, I sense the hopelessness of his situation. He was tall and handsome but inadequate and insufficient. His life came entirely apart at the seams. It continued to only get worse. He could do nothing to turn it around.

He was the problem, and he knew it.

As he grasped the extent of the erosion of his place and watched another rise who was everything he was not, you can only imagine how he felt.

It leaves me surprisingly in sympathy for the enemy of our souls until . . . every thought of him is surpassed by the glorious rise of the one who would eventually become our Saviour.

The villain was lost in the shadow of one who truly answered the desires of the Father's heart.

No wonder that so many years later, the Father would repeatedly rend heaven to proclaim pleasure over His son—His ultimate source of satisfaction.

1 Sam 9-10 | Matt 3:17 | Matt 17:5 | John 12:28

Q1.   Look around in your life. Where do you see the Samuel, Saul and David saga play out with all its drama and contention?

Q2.   Consider your own life and those around you. Do you find yourself embroiled in a similar tale where you are involved in conflict with similar dynamics?

Q3.   Why do you think it is so common for Christians to identify themselves with the life of David?

Prayer.

Lord, whether we find ourselves in the wilderness under threat, or in a palace in peace surrounded by recognition, we acknowledge the Father's desire for righteousness and faithfulness in our lives. In faith we put on Christ as our Jehovah Tsidkenu. In Your presence, we live out of His righteousness and renown. We push forward to be found in him—to be lost within who He was and is. Christ we honour You and savour the flavour of Your heroism and worth—we desire it to soak deeply into our soul. Make us more like You.   Amen.

CHAPTER TWENTY-SEVEN

A FEW GOOD MEN

THEIR COURAGE UNDER FIRE MEANT SO MUCH TO GOD HE ENSURED THEIR STORY IS RETOLD REPEATEDLY.

There you go—we have uncovered the main jist of the Hero, villain and Father scripts. Yet still there is more. God, you see, loves to retell His story. He delights to add layer upon layer until He adequately, in His own mind, portrays each scene.

People are His paint and their lives His canvas, each adding something more to the masterpiece . . .

Think of David on the run and in exile.

Or Job sitting in the dust, at a complete loss.

Or Jesus facing the difficult fact that His life's mission is to give His life away.

Enter the extras! Now, as they take their place on stage, an even more vivid rendering of the backstory of God is revealed before the eyes of a world that is so often lost and in need of a clear reference point.

Each of these had three companions—close companions—a faithful few, whose seemingly minor roles are also not for the faint-hearted.

David had three mighty men who broke through an enemy camp on his behalf. Job also had three men with him, men who put their lives on hold to keep him

1 Sam 21:10 | Job 2:8 | Luke 9 | 2 Sam 23:9-17 | Job 2:11

company as he suffered. And Jesus had Peter, James and John, an inner circle among the disciples. Perhaps it is coincidence, but probably not. Let's run with the pattern here and see where it leads.

These things were done by the three mighty men.

Now Abishai the brother of Joab, the son of Zeruiah, was chief of another three. He lifted his spear against three hundred men, killed them, and won a name among these three. Was he not the most honored of three? Therefore he became their captain. However, he did not attain to the first three.

Now, there's three—plus one! David's three loyal mighty men are accompanied by another mighty champion, one who is next-level in terms of honour and prowess, but somehow he is never exactly included with them as one of the three.

Along the same lines, three men were tossed into a fiery furnace. To our surprise, they didn't die—even though the fire was so hot it incinerated their captor's guards as they manhandled them towards the flames. But then . . .

Suddenly, there's another person in there with them! A glorious figure, like the Son of God! The picture looks a lot like David's three heroes with his 'other champion' . . . the one held in greater honour.

In my mind, this pattern bespeaks characters in the original story—they are, I presume, actually a tribute to the valour of three angels. The idea is that three stood true to the Lord when all was lost in the heavenly rebellion. They overcame their fears, looking total destruction in the face.

Millenia later, a few other good and faithful ones, men this time, find themselves replaying their story, apparently filling their shoes in a similar bind. Nebuchadnezzar was enraged. Three men, Daniel's friends prove faithful, choosing a fiery death rather than idolatry. However, in that fire they experienced a miracle of preservation. And in my mind, I wonder . . . *What if their escape from death was predicated on a similar deliverance in the primeval past?*

Matt 17:1 | Matt 26:36-38 | 2 Sam 23:17-19 | Dan 3:24-30

If so, the script they were on was not the script of the Hero or the villain, but that of the Hero's companions . . . propelling them forward to an assured salvation. Their lives were threatened, but God in His wisdom subtly repositioned them to leverage an aspect of the ultimate epic tale. His intent was to preserve a few of His beloved people. Things got 'hot' for them—a fact used by God to actually guarantee their deliverance! By escalating the threat level, the Lord found a way for them to emerge completely unscathed. His approach allowed for a revelation of His son on earth as the fourth faithful figure in the fire.

It's a question of alignment with the original script . . .

The Father, intoxicated with love for His son, the Hero, is a master at using the scripts to bless his people and honour His son at the same time.

He was there, deeply entrenched in the original tale.

He has first-hand knowledge.

Every nuance of the original story is His to wield.

As we track the story of Shadrach, Meshach and Abednego, we are drawn back to the moment when the Lord and those loyal to Him were targeted for destruction by Lucifer and the rebellious angels. Can you imagine those steadfastly by His side? Can you hear them speak through these words as they echo down the everlasting years to the moment they are recorded in the sacred text?

> *Shadrach, Meshach, and Abed-Nego answered and said to the king, "O Nebuchadnezzar, we have no need to answer you in this matter. If that is the case, our God whom we serve is able to deliver us from the burning fiery furnace, and He will deliver us from your hand, O king. But if not, let it be known to you, O king, that we do not serve your gods, nor will we worship the gold image which you have set up."*

Of course, it is conjecture, but in choosing to believe this is a re-enactment of a primeval story, we gain something extraordinary. The courage of three seemingly insignificant extras in the backstory of God meant so much to God that their story is retold in biblical history. They seem to be an essential part in the mechanism behind the miracle.

Dan 3:16-18

It seems that the best thing to do in a tough season is to find three good friends! And if your friend is the one suffering, why not call a couple of your mates and drop by? In so doing you are making a bold declaration, one which every angel looking on understands, that "this story is not over yet—the tide will turn!"

Let's apply the same idea to the other clear example of the three—Peter, James and John. Watch as the Father uses even the secondary scripts of the extras, to create an atmosphere of affirmation for His precious son in His incarnation.

Jesus was at a watershed moment in His ministry. It was time to turn from the needs of the multitudes to focus on His journey to die in Jerusalem. After fasting for six days, He took three men, His most intimate companions, up onto a mountain. Though He had emptied Himself of all His glory to come to earth, Jesus for a moment was transfigured; to some degree, He connected with His previous state and His place in the original script—and it was glorious!

Then, Moses and Elijah enter the scene and we catch a subtle glimpse of the Father and His son in another time and place when they overcame dire peril. Peter, James and John join the cast as three comrades who stood faithfully with them through that ordeal. Jesus' reaction to the stage that the Father has set for Him is amazing. He is literally caught up in the remembrance, and the power of the retelling is such that His flesh struggles to hold His glory in.

Directly after this event, in fact in the same chapter, we read that Jesus set His face steadfastly to go to Jerusalem. After seeing and experiencing the re-enactment, He was ready to die and fulfil His vital calling. Now He was ready for the greatest challenge of His incarnate life.

Incredibly, three ordinary guys made an important contribution without lifting a finger?

As we scan a wider horizon, we see a larger group—this time there are twelve. They form a pattern too. The image of the three speaks to a poignant moment in a momentous tale, but the twelve seem to warrant close attention too.

Matt 17:1-6 | Luke 9:28-36 | Luke 9:51 | Luke 6:12-16

Joseph's heroic tale includes twelve siblings. Jacob blesses twelve sons. Moses leads twelve tribes. Jesus surrounds Himself with twelve disciples. Later twelve apostles preside over the growth of the church in its infancy.

They fall across the sacred page, diverse in their colour and personality, leaders who share influence in and around the centre of the purposes of God, like ministers in a divine governmental cabinet. And if they too were there in the original tale, it is easy to presume they were rulers in authority. Perhaps they sat around the throne as the elders did millennia later, as described in St John's vision. Their relationship to the Son is immensely important. Where would their loyalties lie? How would they react to the accusation against the Son? When the kingdom they governed was torn asunder, who would they follow, the Hero or the villain?

Most recognise the number twelve as a symbol of authority and government in and of itself, but it appears to borrow this meaning because of its connection to . . . twelve characters in the backstory of God!

Eventually, all twelve tribes of Israel united under King David. This moment of vindication seems to echo another in ages past, when Christ the Son became the chief over twelve who were leaders themselves.

And Joseph weeps for joy. Reunited at last with father and family, we catch a vision of another time and place when the heavenly court emotionally embraced and rallied around the one they had long misunderstood and even spurned. At last, they are confirmed in their devotion to the beloved Son. And in His incarnation, though Christ chose not to call on them, these twelve with the legions under them would have responded to His call—rallying together the armies of the Lord of Hosts they led.

The eleven apostles were conscious of this dynamic in the early chapters of Acts. They believed they could not stand in true authority when one of their number was missing, so they felt compelled to appoint another in Judas' place. Why? Because they realised that even in this age, the success of the venture is bound up in what has gone before, and our attention and alignment to those patterns influences the outworking of God's will on earth.

Gen 49 | Exod 24:4 | Luke 6:12-16 | Acts 1:26 | Rev 4 | 2 Sam 5:1-5 | Gen 43:30
Matt 26:53 | Acts 1:15-26

Q1.   What does the honour associated with the pattern of the three speak to those who might find it difficult to engage directly with a fit in the hero role? Can you relate?

Q2.   When you consider the three and the twelve, where do you find yourself? Do you have an affinity for a Bible character who played in a support role?

Q3.   What do you make of the notion of the heroic community in the purposes of God?

Prayer.

Lord, strengthen us for times when You would have us exalt others and stand with them in their trials. Make us good companions to the faithful as they suffer and faithful ourselves. When we face the fire, clothe us with your zeal and keep us so we do not flinch at the flames. Gather around us a crowd of worshippers ready to risk all for the glory of our Lord Jesus.   Amen.

CHAPTER TWENTY-EIGHT

BAKER'S DOZEN

JAMES THE BROTHER OF OUR LORD STEPS
INTO A POWER VACUUM AND REMARKABLY
TAKES THE HELM.

That reminded me that I had done some research on this before . . .

A lot of what I write sits on the hard drive of my computer; like brewed coffee forgotten too long, I usually discard it for something more recently percolated.

After searching awhile on my backup drive, I found the document I wanted.

I re-read my notes.

They summarised a number of interesting ramifications for our leadership and discipleship approaches today, stemming from a decision made as part of the first Jerusalem council, as recounted in the book of Acts.

James was a lead apostle at the time; he rose and made a call based on the two sides of the debate and his judgement solidified a substantial change in terms of what it meant to be a Gentile (non-Jewish) Christian.

"Yes, there were the twelve. Was this another retelling?"

As I focussed on James, the apparent chair of this council, what coalesced was richer than I'd hoped for.

"Wow! Really? Didn't James die?"

Then it struck me . . .

Acts 15:6

I flicked backward in my Bible and found it a few pages previously.

> *"Then he [Herod] killed James the brother of John with the sword."*

"Which James died?"

"The brother of John—the one we find so often alongside Peter and John, Christ's inner circle in the Gospels, one of the sons of Zebedee?"

"If that James died in Acts twelve, which James do we find leading the church three chapters later?"

"I had just assumed . . ."

"It appears there are two James-es. It could be James the son of Alpheus."

Acts chapter one tells us that the apostles were quick to replace Judas when he died. It also lists who was in the room when that decision was made—eleven apostles along with the women, and Mary the mother of Jesus, *and His brothers.*

"James, the brother of our Lord. Where have I heard those words before . . ?"

> *Then after three years I went up to Jerusalem to see Peter, and remained*
> *with him fifteen days. But I saw none of the other apostles except James,*
> *the Lord's brother.*

In the next chapter, Paul recounts his experience when, fourteen years later, he came to Jerusalem to meet with the apostles.

"Another James—number three! He was on the inside from the early on, alongside Peter. He was also there when Paul visited Peter. It seems to follow that just as Matthias had been chosen to replace Judas, James the brother of our Lord had replaced James the son of Zebedee. In so doing, he not only took his place but also was granted a measure of pre-eminence, a status the original James enjoyed as one of three leaders of the group!"

James number one was dead. Peter needed to lay low because of the threat to his life. John was a leader, but not of the sort with the gift profile required to administer the rapid growth of this unprecedented movement that faced daily challenges from every quarter.

Acts 12:2 I Acts 15:13 I Gal 1:18-19 I Acts 1:14 I Acts 1:15-26

As they filled the gap and added another to their number, the apostles didn't realise the spot had already been filled by Paul—he had already been divinely appointed into their apostolic ranks. And so, when they appoint another, and something remarkable takes place. They thought the number twelve was significant—twelve sons and twelve tribes. What they had not reckoned on, was the amazing potential and power of twelve plus one!

James the brother of our Lord stepped into a power vacuum and remarkably took the helm. Who knew? He rose quickly into his destiny and he is found as the dominant voice in leadership just a few chapters later—he literally had the last word on the discussion! In Acts fifteen, he presided over a meeting of eleven other apostles. Paul was there as well. Paul presents his case, and then, the thirteenth apostle, James, has the final say. It is done. The Jewish and Gentile Christians became one united people in Christ, able to walk in new levels of freedom, and no longer subject to earlier legal, cultural and traditional constraints.

Now, this is exciting! This James was no disciple. He did not fit in. He came late to the party, but amazingly takes a place of pre-eminence. That fits the Hero's story, as we have understood it in previous reflections, but I love the extra nuances we find as we tease out the detail here.

James had really missed out, regrettably part of the entire family of Jesus who thought Him mad and rejected His claims. Only after Christ's death and resurrection do Christ's brothers join those who are loyal to him. The three and a half years he had missed were filled with opportunities, precious experiences and encounters James would never share with the legitimate disciples who had been there throughout the Gospels. On the face of it, this made him ill-equipped to lead—but he did have one thing in his favour, and that was his level of devotion! This particular James was known (probably not to his face) as 'camel-knees.' He had spent so much time at prayer on those knees, that they were noticeably calloused.

Like the Hero Himself, James' devotion prepared him for his unique leadership role—a pivotal position that ended legalistic rule, and restored life and freedom, ushering the kingdom of God into a glorious new day.

Acts 9 | 1 Cor 15:8-11 | Acts 15

Q1.   What is divided in your life needs to be united?

Q2.   How could you take a devoted and heroic posture to facilitate the reestablishment of unity and freedom amongst elements long divided and/or constrained in your world?

Q3.   What apparently random mistake or unintended confluence of events uniquely positions you to lead others into unity of purpose?

Prayer.

Lord, we desire hearts devoted to you, and appetites to seek Your face in prayer. Speak to our confusion so it stumbles us no more, and no longer hinders us from a wholeheartedly emulation of Christ. Prepare us for a lifetime of servant leadership, and free us to walk humbly before our God in freedom and unity.   Amen.

CHAPTER TWENTY-NINE

SKY FALL

I CAN ONLY IMAGINE THE ORIGINAL REALITY WHEN LUCIFER MOVED WITH FURY AGAINST THE FATHER AND HIS SON.

As it turns out, temples and cities are habitually destroyed in scripture. Who would have guessed? The scripts are so powerful they influence where and when cities and temples fall.

We find Samson most famously, with a temple collapsed on top of him, a picture of God under the rubble of His own habitation—the place where angels had once gathered to worship him.

Had God used even a pagan temple to retell His story?

The villain's horrific destruction of Zion was retold repeatedly in the history of the earthly city of God—Jerusalem. The city and its temple took the brunt of the villain's animosity. There is desecration, fire and destruction, time after time . . . because there was desecration, fire and destruction the first time. It's the price the city paid for being and earthly shadow of a heavenly reality.

Solomon built a glorious temple. Then Nebuchadnezzar II besieged Jerusalem in 587 BC and subsequently destroyed it, together with the city. The temple was plundered, burned and destroyed.

Later, Zerubbabel rebuilt it.

Later again, in the Maccabean era, towards the end of the 400 silent years between the testaments, it was literally under fire again, and the desecration described in the books of Maccabees is heart breaking. According to Josephus, the Jews first used fire in the northwest approach to the temple to stop Roman advances. In response, the Romans set fire to an apartment adjacent to the temple. A few bold defenders resisted the desecration of their most holy place. They braved the fire to keep evil out. The attackers added fire of their own to the blaze to defend the holy place, and the temple burned with the defenders within.

Before the birth of Christ, Herod rebuilt Zerubbabel's temple with another more glorious one—a source of Jewish national pride in the oppressive times of the Roman occupation. So treasonous was the sound of Christ's prophesy of its destruction, His words became a key accusation against Him at trial, a little later. Regardless of their palatability, in AD 70 His words came to pass, and the temple was plundered, burned, destroyed and desecrated again.

A pattern emerges, of chaos and bitter catastrophe—a tale of ruin and desolation told over and over—a narrative hard-coded into a fallen creation, repeated to get our attention.

I see three men. Together, they defy an apparently all-powerful monarch, who would have them join his nation's idolatry. They too were engulfed in flames, the flames of a fiery furnace—and pieces of the script mesh together. Something resolves out of the fractals and the fragments . . .

We begin to imagine the scene as Lucifer moves with fury against the Father while three angels brave the flames to guard the holiness of God and His sanctuary. Did devils use the opportunity to then add fire of their own . . . strange fire? We watch from a safe distance across time and space as the temple in heaven is destroyed and the original city of God reduced to rubble.

It was heaven's darkest hour.

Hope faded for the faithful, but suddenly, there was another in the fire—a fourth, like the Son of God! The Hero appears! Then, out of the ashes, they rise.

 Lucifer continues to reign. Heaven begins to rebuild. The Hero and the villain exist in an uneasy relationship until the villain frames the Hero with a lie and the Hero leaves in disgrace.

Josephus 7.1.1 | John 2:20 | Matt 24:1-2 | Matt 26:57-68 | Dan 3:16-30 | Lev 10:1-3

Finally He returns, and we pick up the story . . .

The Hero approaches an apparently invulnerable city, immediately sees a flaw in the defences and prevails effortlessly.

> . . . [they thought], "David cannot come in here." Nevertheless David took the stronghold of Zion (that is, the City of David).

> Now David said on that day, "Whoever climbs up by way of the water shaft and defeats the Jebusites . . . he shall be chief and captain."

> . . And Joab the son of Zeruiah went up first, and became chief.

It is the water shaft that is its vulnerability. Straight in without a fight. Quite a contrast to the utter mess the villain made of Zion in order to get his way. The Hero loved the city, He honoured and protected it, even as he regained it.

Another city and another time retells the same prehistoric event.

A prideful Belshazzar lifted himself up against the Lord of heaven. He bought vessels from the holy temple to his feast and there they drank wine from them, praising the gods of gold, silver, bronze, and iron, wood and stone. Suddenly there was divine writing on the wall and that night his reign and life end.

Cyrus reportedly took the city effortlessly; after the Babylonians retreated into the city, his engineers simply diverted the Euphrates river.

Two effortless battles, both involving vulnerabilities to do with the city's water supply, as a secret means of entering the city.

There is a river in the centre of the glorious city. It flows out from the throne of God to the world outside. The Son returns; His love for the presence and the worship of God have equipped Him with a knowledge of that river. Through it He gained effortless entrance.

Could it be that the fall of these two ancient cities retold the return of the Son to claim His rightful rule and inheritance—His return to one even older?

It was as if the city opened up to allow Him to enter:

2 Sam 5:6-8 | 1 Chron 11:6 | Dan 5 | Herodotus 1.190-191 | Rev 22:1 | Ps 46:4
Ezek 47:1-9

Lift up your heads, O you gates! And be lifted up, you everlasting doors!
And the king of glory shall come in.

But this is a tale of *two* cities, and now it is time to turn our attention to the *other* city, with a narrative pattern slightly different in plot-line, but equally of note.

Joshua took Jericho. He built no earthen siege ramps. He had no ladders, battering rams or towers. They just circle in a choreographed pattern and then blow trumpets at exactly the correct time, and the city walls just fall down— just like that. His entrance into the city is unexpectedly effortless.

How?

It's the scripts again.

The Hero reigns, but elsewhere, Lucifer has fled. He has fortified his position in a city of his own.

Christ goes out against him and the city. If heaven is ever to enjoy peace again, this evil archangel must be defeated and cast down!

The Hero comes with the host of heaven. They march and hold trumpets, but before them a group of angels leads the way carrying something important. In Joshua's day the ark of the covenant was the prop to convey an ancient reality that may be better understood if we consider a palanquin holding the centre of heaven's worship Himself—conveniently, these vehicles look remarkably similar to the ark of the covenant. At the Hero's request, the Father joins the fray. He is carried within and hidden behind the palanquin's curtains, and His powerful presence becomes part of the equation. As trumpets rouse him, He acts, and the very fabric of the city walls rebels against the villain as it is called back into line with the Father's will. The villanous city falls. The Hero and the Father ascend in glory and victory, and the land is cleansed of evil.

Ps 24:7 | Josh 6

Q1.   Have you ever been under the rubble? What have you built only to have it destroyed, broken and/or burned with fire?

Q2.   The Devil was a murderer from the beginning. What else was he back then?

Q3.   The destruction of Jerusalem and the Exile came as a shock in 586BC. If you used the scripts, how would you explain to the Jews then what had just happened to them?

Prayer.

Lord, we value Your holiness, the sacred space You inhabit and the worship of Your name. We draw near to stand in the consuming fire to contend for Your presence. Though the enemy comes in like a flood, we seek You in the confusion and loss, aware that once a similar attack was laid at Your feet as well. Support us to represent You well.   Amen.

CHAPTER THIRTY

REBUILD THE RUINS

I CAN ONLY IMAGINE THE ORIGINAL REALITY
WHEN LUCIFER MOVED WITH FURY AGAINST
THE FATHER AND HIS SON.

A n obscure verse in the book of Joshua speaks directly to the story of the Hero, the villain and the Father. It plays out in the context of the reconstruction of the city and the temple.

> *Then Joshua charged them at that time, saying, "Cursed be the man*
> *before the Lord who rises up and builds this city Jericho; he shall lay*
> *its foundation with his firstborn, and with his youngest he shall set*
> *up its gates."*

As far as I can deduce, at the moment of outright attack and catastrophe, the subject of the previous chapter, two things occurred.

Firstly, the Father experienced Lucifer's blatant betrayal. Lucifer was lost to him, and that was felt like the loss of a firstborn son (Christ is and was the Father's only Son. There is no inference here to suggest Lucifer was actually a son in any sense of the word—instead, the experience of his loss to the Father felt like the loss of a son. This scene is often retold in these terms).

The villain destroys Zion, the city is sacked and ruined—there is desecration, destruction and fire. Lucifer has targeted the Lord Himself. The Father, the Son and the faithful survive the attack. Amazingly, even though his attack was unsuccessful and his intentions were now clear, his darkening reign continued.

Josh 6:26

The interplay between Saul, David, God and Samuel is useful here. The villain is not lost and gone for good, not cast down as he will be in the end. He still holds power because of the immutability of his anointing. However, the relationship between him and the Father is irreparably damaged. Similarly, Saul blew it, and God moved on. David would take his place. David holds to the promise on his life while Saul continues reign in ways that continue to irritate and disappoint the Lord more and more.

In the book of Esther, Xerxes (a type of the Father) is attacked in an attempted assassination attempt. It is unsuccessful and Mordechai (a type of the Son) is credited with the preservation of his life.

The betrayal, and attempted assassination of God is unsuccessful. The Hero (the Son) makes an entrance and somehow thwarts it. Lucifer intended to simply seize power and rid Himself of the Father. Instead, he lives on and the effect of his attack is to completely undermine the mandate of his continued reign. The Father moved on emotionally. As the rebuild begins, Lucifer has become effectively dead to the Father.

The rebuild is a time of contention between the Son and Lucifer, mirrored in the lives of Saul and David. One fades and the other rises.

It appears the rebuild was a time of threat but not outright conflict between a divided kingdom. Nehemiah rebuilds with a sword in one hand and a trowel in the other. My guess is, the fall of the temple and city were significant, and the seat of power with Lucifer at its head had already moved elsewhere. The faithful rebuilt. The Son led the effort. When the walls, gates and bars are set up, Sabbath rest ensues—the faithful have a refuge from the rest of the kingdom—they with their love for commerce are shut out. The Hero is gaining status with this incredible victory.

The Son's success in restoring order must have gladdened the heart of God the Father. In response, Lucifer turns to a lie and an accusation (hence Christ's offhand statement, ". . .the devil . . . was a murder from the beginning, and does not stand in the truth, because there is no truth in him"). The Son was framed by the villain. How utterly foreign that first ever lie was. Only truth had existed until that moment. The Father was taken unawares, just like Potiphar was by

1 Sam 16 | Esther 6 | Neh 4:15-18 | Neh 13:17-22 | John 8:44

his wife's accusation of Joseph, which undoubtedly also helps us understand the nature of the original lie in focus here.

Judas' betrayal leads quickly to a kangaroo court, full of false accusation.

The Son in His original and greatest story was falsely accused and then exiled into a time of loneliness and isolation.

Zion's gates had just been set up. It was time to celebrate all that had been restored, but from the Father's perspective, He had just incurred another tragic loss. He had lost another son. Here is the curse over Jericho restated:

> " . . . he shall lay its foundation with his firstborn, and with his youngest
> he shall set up its gates."

The people of God fell on hard and oppressive times. There was never enough, just want and disappointment.

In the book of Haggai, there is a biblical account of the people of God as they rebuild the temple. The economy is in tatters, and the blessings they have known are forgotten amidst a time of constant disappointments and unrealised expectations.

It wasn't just that Lucifer was at the helm. It was that *the rebuild was unfinished!*

The gates had been restored. The security of the city of God had been re-established, but the temple remained as a pile of rubble. Satan's great and terrible lie had prevented the Son from one final and important work—the repair of the heart of worship for the people of God.

There was law. There was commerce. But there was no place for the Father to call home in this restored city.

In the catastrophe, disobedience and idolatry had reached a peak. It culminated in a moment where a prophet once watched as the presence of God left the temple and moved away from Jerusalem.

In Haggai, how was the curse that devoured the prosperity of the people countered? That's right. The temple was rebuilt.

Gen 39:16-20 | Josh 6:26 | Haggai 1:3-11 | Ezek 10 | Haggai 2:18-23

Those very dynamics tie that story to the original one, when the Son returned, welcomed with delight by the Father. The Hero understands that worship is the essential heartbeat of heaven and that His father inhabits praise, so He rebuilds—He's making a home for His father to dwell in.

The Son rebuilds the temple, and that time is pictured by Zerubbabel the governor and Joshua the high priest, working together on a temple restoration project.

Are these two the Father and Son at work together—driven by their shared love for worship, the life-blood of the people of God!

When the prophet Haggai retells the story, from the moment the foundations were laid, blessing is possible again. Why? What was in play, to make this happen?

With the rebuild the Father had a place again. The temple restored brought with it the return of the presence, joy and the life of God to the city, together with all the blessings He routinely releases over the lives of His loved ones. As the Son re-establish the seat of worship He refounded the economy and brought an end to the work of the influence of the devourer and the plunderer in that place.

The point is this. With the reconstruction comes a return of hope and prosperity.

The Son is at the helm of heaven. It is a time of abundance and prosperity!

How was the Son allowed back? How could He be restored to the Father's side in light of the accusations Lucifer had brought against him? Was Jesus recounting this moment when He told the story of the prodigal son?

The answer lies in another book of the Bible. While Haggai retells the rise of the people to rebuild the ruined temple, Zachariah shares a perspective on an intimate moment.

In Zechariah, Satan is pictured. He stands there accusing Joshua—but the accuser finds himself rebuked, and Joshua the High Priest is forgiven, restored and re-clothed with honour.

Luke 15:11-32 | Zech 3

Joshua's iniquity (the false accusations) are taken away. His filthy clothes are removed and clothes of office are put on and he is anointed to serve and govern and to take charge of the courts of the Lord.

And so, Joseph leaves the prison for the palace. Mordachai is honoured, David leaves the service of Achish, the Philistine king of Gath. Jeroboam returns from exile in Egypt.

And the Hero comes home to Zion.

This is the end of a dramatic scene in the hero script. It began as a lie, and an accusation against the Son.

Finally He is vindicated.

His exile comes to an end. He is welcomed back into intimacy with the Father. The city and temple are restored, and at last, the Hero takes the position and place the villain once held!

Then and now, the people welcomed the rule and reign of the Son—the one righteous and glorious leader.

But for the Son, the best is yet to come!

Gen 41:9-44 | Esther 6 | 1 Sam 29:9-10 | 1 Kings 12:1-3

Q1.   Have you ever experienced a purse with holes, where you continually find less than you thought you had stored away?

Q2.   How have you proven the power and significance of worship as a force for transformation of negative situations in your life?

Q3.   When have you been vindicated, and how do you further long for God to act in this way in your life?

Prayer.

Lord, we agree with Your estimation of Christ—worthy to govern and take charge of every aspect of our lives. We value His rule and reign, and long for Him to transform all the broken down pieces in our personal and public lives. Christ, You draw us into the sanctuary and lead us into the presence. We lose ourselves in the Father's love and joy, and stand aside to allow You to bring our lives into order.   Amen.

CHAPTER THIRTY-ONE

OPPRESSION AND DIVISION

IF OUR WORDS AND ACTIONS DESTROY LIVES
AND REPUTATIONS, HAVE WE INADVERTENTLY
ALLOWED OURSELVES TO BECOME PAWNS.

When Solomon completes the temple it represents the highest and most glorious point of the hero script. The shekinah glory fell—a cloud so thick the priest could no longer function in their roles . . .

As we pursue clarity on what happened in the very beginning it is useful to reflect on Solomon's later years.

They were not so glorious.

Not many years after he typifies Christ at His most majestic, we find Solomon slipping from that wonderful ideal, becoming an oppressive ruler. His heart turned from the Lord to foreign wives and their idolatory. He used people as forced labour—a characteristic of villainous rather than heroic leadership. It was unfortunate for those around them, and a shame to him personally. Solomon, the one who played the part of the Hero in His greatest moment of glory, was unable to sustain his alignment with the hero script.

Towards the end, he slowly lost his way. At this latter time of his life, Solomon (and Rehoboam, his son after him), typified the hard-hearted villain. Enter Jeroboam, who plays the Hero in this retelling.

Solomon, found him to be industrious and appointed him over a significant proportion of his labour force. Jeroboam is anointed and Solomon finds out, and we have the dynamics of Saul and David repeated once more—in his

2 Chron 7:1-3 | 1 Kings 11:1-4 | 1 Kings 9:15-22 | 1 Kings 11:26-28

version, David flees into exile in the wilderness, and in his adaptation, Jeroboam runs for his life and lives as an exile in Egypt.

Jeroboam finally returns to find a people pushed beyond the brink of what they can bear. The oppression is too much and they have begun to reject Rehoboam's authority.

The kingdom is divided. Jeroboam, like the Hero before him, returns from exile to dispossess a king whose glory had eroded into idolatry and futility.

There is a lesson here . . .

Beginning on one script or the other does not guarantee a particular destination. Like Solomon, we can slide from one to the other in both redemptive or regrettable ways.

The ancient saga of the Hero and the villain is retold through all our lives. When the Hero arrives, a season of oppression comes to an end.

Two leadership styles that are diametrically opposed—they couldn't be more different, and in that contrast we find ourselves bowed in worship, eyes fixed on the wonder of the Son as the perfect leader.

Compare Moses and Joshua, and a similar comparison can be seen.

Moses leads a people, hungry and thirsty. As they cross a desert with only enough food for the day, they complain and wander. Finally they come to a place of fear and awe . . . and laws are given as they revel in idolatry.

Another leader rises to take Moses' place. He leads the people into a land of milk and honey. They take their inheritance and eat of the abundance of the land. Joshua, the hero, leads them into victory!

Moses was a good man, a man of God. And we don't look at things this way to slight him in the least, but as we lean into the original story we find a subtle echo of a past oppressive, legalistic period, and the comparison continues as in his anger he fell out of step with God and was replaced.

1 Sam 21:10 | 1 Kings 11:40 | Exod 15-Deut 34 | Josh 1-19 | Num 20:7-12 | Deut 31:1-2

What came next was freedom, victory and joy as the Son came to power, typified by Joshua (who happens to have the same name as the Son would have, later in His incarnation).

For us today, it is important to journey in our hearts, minds and lives from a life as orphans and slaves, to become lavishly blessed sons and daughters of God. This is the flavour of the reign of Christ, before the beginning, then and also now.

Oppressive thought pervades the theology of the global church; even after millennia of the development of Christian thought, I hear the echo of those difficult years before time began—like the crack of a thousand whips.

Graceless sermons bow down the backs of the people of God, just as they did when a Pharaoh demanded bricks without straw! Harsh depreciating lectures only serve to supress and depress those who God delights to build up and welcome into joy.

Let's cease and desist from using our pulpits as soap boxes for the villain's lies.

Christ the Son has come. The liar and the accuser has been silenced!

Let's muffle guilt-laced allegations and welcome the truth of unconditional love and irrepressible hope.

Ransomed, healed, restored, forgiven!

> Blameless in His sight . . .

Let's stand and refuse to agree with "theology" perpetrated by the enemy of our souls?

Here is a clue. What does the villain think of humanity?

> Nothing good, that's for sure.

In the book of Job, one of his companions is visited by horror—it's the night before he "comforts" his friend whose life has fallen apart. Not only is Satan the cause of Job's problems. He is also in the ears of those who could encourage him through this terrible time.

John 1:12 | John 14:18 | Gal 4:6 | Ex 5:6-7 | Rev 12:10-11 | Eph 1:4 | Job 4:12-21

His poison pervades the atmosphere as he provides a debilitating assessment of Job and his circumstances.

He is in bed. In the darkness of the night a horrific visitor comes. Eliphaz, Job's friend, is full of dread and his whole body trembles. It is a spirit . . . obviously an evil spirit, and I believe the villain himself. Eliphaz's bones shake. He is terrified, and the hairs on the back of his neck stand on end.

So what does the deceiver have to say over the situation?

> *"People are impure, not trusted by God, or worth noticing. They are easily broken and they quickly perish and die without wisdom."*

Nothing positive to say at all. Just one put-down after the next.

If what we have to say is along the same lines, have we just become a spokesman for the opposition? If our words and actions destroy lives and reputations, have we inadvertently allowed ourselves to become pawns in the hands of the one who detests and despises humankind? He desires to have us, but we must master the evil before the darkness becomes our master, using our authority for its own purposes.

Job 4:16-21 | Gen 4:7

Q1.   What is oppressive in your life? Is it from God? Do you believe it is His will for you?

Q2.   Is there anything oppressive about your words or actions towards others?

Q3.   What is the answer to oppression, both perpetrated against you or by you?

Prayer.

Lord, set us free, and bring healing, freedom and deliverance to those around as well. Surround us with songs of deliverance, empowered and enabled to break through fear, guilt and bitter anger. Remake us according to Your loving kindness and lead us forth in peace. Make us an instrument of Your peace we pray.   Amen.

CHAPTER THIRTY-TWO

COMMUNITIES IN CONFLICT

THEY COME OUT FROM UNDER THE
TYRANNY OF A DARK KINGDOM, GRACE IS
EXTENDED TO THEM IN ABUNDANCE.

The concentric circles of cast-members that support the lead roles are ever-widening. The Hero and the Father. Then the three and beyond them, then the twelve, and around them, a community of the faithful.

The Son reigns and prosperity is restored as one by one, His enemies fall at the Hero's feet, subdued.

Meanwhile, elsewhere, the villain regroups his strength.

In these times the faithful are referred to in scripture as the remnant (e.g. Obadiah keeps the faithful hidden safe in a cave), the few who remain faithful regardless of the opposition or cost.

In the story of Joseph, a parallel narrative finds a nation under the leadership of a hero. They enjoy seven years of plenty.

Elsewhere, however, there is famine and distress—two very different realities at the same time.

A divided kingdom.

Communities in conflict.

You guessed it. We could take a closer look at Judah and Israel as they were divided in a long drawn out and bitter rivalry.

1 Cor 15:25 | Isa 10-11 | 1 Kings 18:1-4 | Gen 41 | 1 Kings 12-2 Kings 25

Or, the book of Judges which retells a similar era, could be our reference.

Against a backdrop of the legitimate rule of the Son, guerrilla war morphs into outright civil war . . . famine, pestilence, forced labour, suffering and pain. The destroyer destroys. The devourer devours. The liar lies.

Slavery. The ten plagues. Hunger. Loss. Seven years of hardship, until those who have followed the villain turn from him to the refuge of the Hero's reign.

He has faithfully laid aside provision in the years of plenty, and there is enough for all.

The twelve are reunited with the Son they rejected. Their previously legitimate leader turned sour. Finally, they recognise the fact—only pain follows those loyal to Lucifer.

For the first time since the rebellion of Lucifer, the kingdom is united again; this is typified in David's life as he reigned, first over two tribes, and later over the entire kingdom as it was united under him.

This is not the end of the story. The divided kingdom after Solomon's reign puts flesh on the bones of the narrative first played out before the beginning of time. There was a schism. Judah and Israel were at loggerheads and the conflict dragged on. Idolatry brought a curse along with hardship and vulnerability. Yes, indeed! Suddenly we find ourselves dusting of the books of Kings, studying the ebbs and flows between two rival kingdoms and their rulers that personify at times, both the Hero and villain in powerful contest.

Until something gives, and the fallen repent and return, coming out from under the tyranny of a dark kingdom—grace is extended to them in abundance.

So, the Gentiles are welcomed into the early church and it is utterly amazing! These pagans coming in from the cold are not subject to a bunch of restrictions. The Holy Spirit indwells them and equips them so their lives are dramatically transformed. They too get the experience of leaving captivity and bondage, and being welcomed into freedom, rest and joy.

It's not just grace that welcomes those with a dark past.

Judges 1 | Ex 7-12 | Gen 41 | 2 Sam 1-5 | 1 Kings 12-2 Kings 25 | Acts 10-15

It is *powerful grace,* a force that awakens a rebel heart to a love for righteousness. It is a *restorative grace* that binds those who are broken in spirit and renews them as if they had been created afresh.

War ceases and unity is re-established, under the reign of the glorious Son.

The scales have tipped and power rests in the hand of the Son, but some continue to resist . . .

And so, Israel as a nation would not enter in. They would not submit to the rule and reign of Christ as the church was forming. Regardless of their status at times in the past as the faithful community, these choices serve to transport them as a community onto the villain script, or at least to align them with the script of the community of those who followed the villain at this time now in our focus.

They are found in conflict with the faithful, the church, however, the original tale speaks a promise into the division and imbibes hope of a final reunification.

This delightful fact provides the mechanism behind their future restoration.

It is the means whereby they can be received again into the fold, grafted back in.

This is how God will get it done! Again, the power of these mighty scripts will provide a fabric for the will of God to be worked out in this world.

The amazing act of grace in the future of God's original earthly people referred to as the hope of Israel, relies on the scripts as well.

They have a future because there is a precedent of a rebellious people once long lost to God being welcomed back in.

John 1:16 | Acts 4:33 | 1 Peter 5:10-12 | Rom 9-11

Q1.   Have you lost hope for any communities or groups in your life because of their behaviour?

Q2.   Is there a way you can provide a welcome for them into redemption, freedom and/or salvation?

Q3.   Are you part of a remnant community? What is the future of the true and faithful company?

Prayer.

Lord, put Your hand on us so we appreciate Your grace in the lives of others around us. We desire to be channels for Your redemptive purposes as You lead many sons to glory. Let us be gatekeepers in the house of the Lord, so we can open the door wide and usher in everyone ready to enter.   Amen.

CHAPTER THIRTY-THREE

ENDGAME

_____

THE HERO IS PRAISED BY ALL. HE LIVES IN TRIUMPH, AND IS THE CENTRE OF THE JOY OF THE FATHER.

In the end, the Hero and the villain take hold of their contrasting destinies. The Hero, once so humbled, now rises from glory to glory. The villain, in his pride, overreached and fell.

His end was final and horrible, and all who followed his lead experienced the same. Saul falls on the sword. Haman hangs on the gallows. Absalom hangs from a tree. So did Judas, in an amazingly terrible but apparently predictable coincidence.

Each villain's plans unravelled until they fell irretrievably.

> *"How you are fallen from heaven, O Lucifer, son of the morning! How you are cut down to the ground, You who weakened the nations!"*

> *"I saw Satan fall like lightning from heaven"*

> *. . . a great, fiery red dragon . . . His tail drew a third of the stars of heaven and threw them to the earth . . . the great dragon was cast out, that serpent of old, called the Devil and Satan, who deceives the whole world; he was cast to the earth, and his angels were cast out with him.*

The enemy and those who refused to turn back from him are now gone at last. Heaven rejoices and peace is restored. The Hero is praised by all. He lives in triumph, and is the centre of the joy of the Father.

1 Sam 31:1-5 | Esther 7:10 | 2 Sam 18:9-15 | Matt 27:5 | Isa 14:12 | Luke 10:18
Rev 12:3-9

And they all lived happily ever after.

It is the way all good stories end.

They all entered into rest.

The first sabbath brought the hero script to a close.

And just when we think this is the best place to leave things, something else happens.

The story breaks out of the reality of heaven,

into the shadowlands far from there,

The story is retold.

Creation sets up the backdrop,

and the rest is history, literally.

The scripts were written into the fabric of space and time. A faithful few, hand in hand with the Son, known as Jehovah at that time, found a way to honour His original legacy with Him as guide.

Pagan multitudes grappled in the dark. They died confused at the apparently haphazard nature of the circumstances of their life.

Jehovah lends His aid again. His fingers write in stone. The light of law came to illuminate the elemental forces that governed the cause and effect of humanity. The people of God rejoiced at these precepts and wisdom, a gift from above.

Surely the Hero had done enough, but no, He would do more.

Now, it was time for the incarnation.

Just like in 1977, when the boxing legend Mohamed Ali played the lead role in his autobiography adapted for cinema,

The Hero was cast as Himself!

Christ comes in human form to play *Himself*, in the role of the Hero.

Rom 2 | Ps 119:97, 105 | John 1:1-18 | 1 John 1-4

The mechanics of the Earth lend Him aid in His quest to rescue another community—human rather than angelic—also held for such a long time in bondage.

To come, He must start again, He must become humble. He would empty Himself, divinity laid aside. Thankfully, humility was a practiced art for the faithful Son.

And so, humanity saw the face of God, and they beheld His glory, the glory as of the only begotten of the Father, full of grace and truth.

Eventually He would pray and ask the Father to restore to Him the glory He had before the world was.

For the glory set before Him He endured . . .

Eventually He rose, and ascended and was enthroned again.

Now He reigns, labouring humbly and faithfully, until all that grieves the heart of His father is put down. Then He will stand aside, hand the throne and sceptre back, and we are left with a sense of longing and anticipation—when every aspect of heaven and earth resonates with the beauty of the Father's heart and true sabbath is restored once more.

Phil 2:1-11 | Matt 11:29 | John 1:14 | 1 John 1:2 | Heb 12:2 | 1 Cor 15:20-28

Q1.   If the scripts govern your life, what should change for you?

Q2.   How does the original story inform your worship of Christ?

Q3.   The incarnation, seen in light of the original script welcomes us into similar humility. How can you share the mind of Christ in the weeks to come?

Prayer.

Lord. We still ourselves in Your presence in awe of Your heart and mind. We consider the end of all things and feel a change in ourselves to bear all things, believe all things, hope all things and endure all things. Draw us, Father into Your presence and shape us so we are ready for Your eternal bliss.   Amen.

HERO WORSHIP

For He Himself is our peace, who has made both one, and has broken down the middle wall of separation, having abolished in His flesh the enmity, that is, the law of commandments contained in ordinances, so as to create in Himself one new man from the two, thus making peace, and that He might reconcile them both to God in one body through the cross, thereby putting to death the enmity. And He came and preached peace to you who were afar off and to those who were near. For through Him we both have access by one Spirit to the Father.

Now, therefore, you are no longer strangers and foreigners, but fellow citizens with the saints and members of the household of God, having been built on the foundation of the apostles and prophets, Jesus Christ Himself being the chief cornerstone, in whom the whole building, being fitted together, grows into a holy temple in the Lord, in whom you also are being built together for a dwelling place of God in the Spirit.

Ephesians 2:14-22

Shadrach, Meshach, and Abednego in the Fiery Furnace

This preeminent tale undergirds the earth beneath our feet. It is the essence of wisdom, law and grace. It is a lamp to our feet and a light to our path.

To the Jews, the law illuminated the two divergent scripts—blessing and curse, favour and prosperity, righteousness and truth.

The book of Proverbs resonates with the wisdom of the scripts. As the life and perspective of Solomon, the 'wisest man who ever lived,' aligned with those scripts, the result was truly glorious.

Hidden amongst those precepts, in Proverbs chapter eight, Solomon describes the architect of creation, the Holy Spirit, alongside the original Hero, delighting in him, exuding joy and guiding the work of the Hero's fingers as He shapes the world.

In hindsight, it is clear that what the Holy Spirit was intent on doing, was weaving the script into creation. Script and backstory formed the primary design paradigm that undergirded everything they made.

Later, when Christ comes, His adeptness with the scripts releases two gifts to humanity. He gives His long-time companion, the Holy Spirit who is the very personification of wisdom, to accompany us. He is the ultimate guide for us in life, the one who can truly instruct our hearts to find the pathway of blessing and resist evil. The Holy Spirit writes the hero script deep into the fabric of our hearts and sets us up for a lifetime of favour with heaven and earth—an unattainable ideal for Solomon as he penned his proverbs.

And secondly, we are welcomed in, given a hero's welcome. We come before the Father to experience all the lavish love He has for the one who always pleased Him in every way. We are 'in the beloved,' and we will spend the rest of our eternal life on a quest to search out the full significance of those words!

All we experience hinges on principles of dispossession. The precedent of the Hero's dispossession of the villain becomes a primary means to empower all the blessings Christ releases to us.

The New Testament teaches us that we cannot get on-script by ourselves. We need help!

Dispossession is required,

>	and it's fruits cannot be received without humility.

We stoop.

>	We find our knees.

>		We know we cannot play the hero in and of ourselves.

And we admit,

"Lord, we are bankrupt. Left to ourselves we are hellbent on our own destruction. Without Your divine intervention we have such a strong affinity to the lifestyle of the villain, so help us, we pray."

Without dispossession we are left in bondage.

Without this precious dynamic, we are mere law keepers—earthbound orphans and slaves trying to reach for an allusive and unattainable standard—instead of sons and daughters who enjoy the delights of the Father's house and heart.

We need Jesus, so very much.

We need the Hero to intervene—not just for salvation, but to find healing and identity and freedom. We need Christ to lend us all that He deserves and take away all that we naturally deserve.

We need Jesus.

We need to embrace Him and dispossess Him of all that is His by right.

He meets us there.

In His embrace we find freedom from sin, bondage, brokenness and all the consequences we rightfully deserve.

We stand beneath the cross and see His suffering and humiliation. It is all well-deserved, though not by Him.

And we worship, filled with thankfulness.

Until at last, He takes us deeper still.

As we take His place and position we realise we are heirs of so much more.

Our relationship with the heroic Son is far more intimate and powerful than we could ever have imagined.

The next section reflects on what it means to live as heirs of all things in Christ, completely lost in the life of the Hero, the beloved Son of God manifest in us and the resulting tangible expression of God's will that brings forth into our lives.

PART
4

INTIMACY AND
AUTHORITY

HERO WORSHIP

Men of Israel, hear these words: Jesus of Nazareth, a Man attested by God to you by miracles, wonders, and signs which God did through Him in your midst, as you yourselves also know— Him, being delivered by the determined purpose and foreknowledge of God, you have taken by lawless hands, have crucified, and put to death; whom God raised up, having loosed the pains of death, because it was not possible that He should be held by it.

Acts 2:22-24

The Triumph of Mordechai

CHAPTER THIRTY-FOUR

YOUR BLESSING DAY

RUN INTO THE FOREST AND ROLL
AROUND IN THE MUCK AND FOLIAGE
UNTIL YOU SMELL LIKE JESUS.

You are asleep. The blinds are drawn, and the room is dark in spite of the arrival of dawn outside. Suddenly, you are shaken awake . . . not roughly, but with some urgency. There is excitement in the Holy Spirit's voice,

"Come quickly! It's your blessing day!"

"What's going on?"

"Your father has chosen today. He will bless one of His children today and that child will be you!"

"But . . ."

"But nothing. Get dressed quickly. We need to work fast!"

In minutes, you are through the shower and dressed and you find the Holy Spirit in the kitchen. The shower has left your hair wet and your mind clear.

"You make no sense! You know how this works. Father loves Jesus. He's the eldest and He will get all the blessings."

"Not today. Jesus left early—before dawn. He won't be back for ages. He went on a hunt, so He could prepare a meal for your father."

"We just need to be quick . . ."

Gen 27:1-6

"This doesn't sound very smart to Me . . ."

"Listen. We don't have time. Go quickly and find the best goat you have in your flock. Skin it and bring Me the meat as fast as you can. Hurry!"

You run down the path to the barn, full of worry about where this will all lead.

"Curly or Puddles? Which would taste better? Oh, of course. It must be Bessy. She is younger still, so her meat will be tenderer."

You snatch Bessy from the flock and return to the house in haste. You find the Holy Spirit in the kitchen in a hive of activity. There are chopped vegetables on the bench and a sauce simmers over the gas burner. Spices bottles and boxes of herbs are scattered all around. He is hard at work, grinding them together in a mortar and pestle.

"Ahh. You're back. Great! Do you have the goat meat?"

"Yes. I kept it on the bone."

"Good. Now listen."

You look up in apprehension and He takes you by the shoulders.

"Trust me, child. I know what I'm about and believe Me, this is the only way for you to be blessed. It has been in My heart for years but now we have the opportunity. Come on, we have to get you in costume."

"Costume?"

"Yes, the Father must think you are Jesus . . ."

"But I can't. It's impossible. There is no possible way the Father would think I am Jesus."

"Difficult, yes, but not impossible, child. It doesn't matter how you look, but it matters a great deal how you feel and smell. Your father does not look on the outward appearance. He is blind to how you appear. Just tie the goatskin on your arms and legs, go run into the forest and then roll around in the muck and foliage until you smell like Jesus."

Gen 27:8-17

Twenty minutes later, you are back in the kitchen, out of breath and bathed in sweat. Your mind is a mess of fear and confusion.

"Just wonderful. Let Me feel your arms."

The Holy Spirit reaches out and sighs with satisfaction. He bends down and inhales deeply through his nose. Another sigh and a cheeky grin, altogether frightening under the circumstances.

The oven dings loudly and the Holy Spirit turns and pulls an oven mitt onto his right hand. Pulling a dish from within the oven, He lays it on a board on the bench and continues to speak as He prepares the plate of food.

"This is your destiny, My child. It is how it's meant to be. The only thing between your future and you is a simple act of courage. You are in costume, just remember to stay in character. You have put on Christ, but you need to take on his identity entirely if this is to work! Believe Me . . . I know your father's tastes like no other. He will enjoy this dish. This will be great. What's more, look at you! You are ready. Everything is ready. Go take this dish to Him."

Gen 27:17 | Rom 13:14 | Gal 3:27

Q1.   We used to talk about, "What would Jesus do?" How is the Christian life an exercise in Jesus impersonation?

Q2.   How do you feel when you are about to come before the Father?

Q3.   What does it mean to you when you read Galatians as it encourages us to 'put on Christ'?

Prayer.

Lord. We want to be conformed to the image of Your Son, but we feel like imposters. Holy Spirit, we submit to Your kind ministrations as You prepare us to stand before the Father, as You position us to receive His lavish blessings. Heal and cleanse our minds and hearts. Loose the shackles of our confidence and expectations so they are unbound, and transform us so we are in every way—body, soul and spirit—in the Beloved.   Amen.

CHAPTER THIRTY-FIVE

BEFORE THE FATHER

HIS LOVE REACHES OUT TO YOU AS IT
NEVER HAS BEFORE. THIS IS HOW
JESUS MUST FEEL ALL THE TIME.

Shaking a little, you make your way down the hallway and knock on the door. The knock seems louder than usual. After all, what would Jesus do, right?

"Come in, child. I am ready for My meal."

You step forward with the bowl, arm outstretched as though a barrier between you and your Dad might be a good idea.

"My father."

"Here I am. Who are you, My son?"

"I am Jesus, Your firstborn."

You can't believe you really said those words. You never thought that invoking the name of Jesus would come to this! You have come so far with the charade that who you are in this moment seems uncertain, even to yourself.

"I have done as You told me; now sit and eat my game. It's time for You to bless me."

"Hmm. Something sure smells good, but how were you so quick? I would have thought you would take a few more hours."

Gen 27:18-25

"Sure, you're right, Dad, but God helped me. He made it so much easier."

"Really?"

He turns His head to the side as if perplexed. The open door behind you grows ever more inviting with every passing second.

"Come close; let Me feel your arms. I want to make sure you are really Jesus."

He reaches out and strokes the goatskin with His fingers.

"It's really quite strange," He says, bewildered. "You have the arms of Jesus, but your voice is as if it belongs to another. Are you really Him?"

"I am!"

Your father sighs contentedly. His apprehensions are stilled. He places his hand on your shoulder and begins to bless you . . .

"See, the smell of my child is as the smell of a fertile and blessed field! May you have the dew of heaven and of the fullness of the earth and plenty of grain and wine. Let others serve you, and nations bow down to you. Be lord over your brothers and sisters. May they bow down to you as well. Cursed be everyone who curses you and blessed be everyone who blesses you!"

As He speaks, you look up into His wrinkled face and see so much affection written there. His love reaches out to you as it never has before. "This is how Jesus must feel all the time," you think to yourself.

The kindness in His unseeing eyes and the words He declared have gotten under your skin.

You feel your emotions rise . . .

He pauses .

"You have all I have to give. You have it all, beloved child. Now, how about some of your stew?"

The bowl has grown heavy during the long wait and you gladly hand it over. Your pulse races as you watch Him eat.

Gen 27:18-29

It's done! The Holy Spirit was right. It was not impossible! Wow!

Your elation is shattered, however, as a realisation of the sheer magnitude of the possible consequences of your actions envelops all conscious thought.

"What about the real Jesus? This is way beyond blasphemy! I'm as good as dead. I have dispossessed Christ Himself!"

Thanking your father, you leave hurriedly and then you run, far, fast and hard. Your legs burn, and your lungs cry out in pain—terror drives you on until the darkness of the night swallows the path and you can go no further.

You are far from home.

Emotionally and physically exhausted you fall to the ground. You could sleep anywhere tonight—a helpful fact, because where you lie is the only choice you have. Even a rock for a pillow seems a strange but attractive invitation. Sleep comes upon you quickly and for hours you are held deeply in its embrace.

And then, suddenly, you awake with a start.

It is the middle of the night, but things are bright, and you seem surrounded by unfamiliar noises.

As you look around you let out a loud gasp!

Angels! A great many angels, in fact.

They're walking up and down a translucent staircase, just metres away from where you have been asleep—a staircase that winds up and up as if it goes all the way to heaven.

It never occurs to you that this celestial demonstration is about you and what you have done this very day. You think you have stumbled on a special sacred place.

But they are not here because of a place.

They are here for you.

Gen 27:30-28:22

They have come to deliver the blessings your father, just hours before, released over you and your life.

Hooray!

It's your blessing day.

Q1.   Reflect on the chapter and the spiritual dynamic of dispossession. How far is too far when it comes to your impersonation of Christ?

Q2.   What does it mean to you to invoke the name of Jesus? Is His name your authority or your identity?

Q3.   What would it take for you step boldly into your full authority and standing in Christ?

Prayer.

Lord. We want to be found in Christ, with a righteousness not our own. We long to become an epicentre of the kingdom and a conduit out of which the blessings of the Father interface with a fallen world. Bless us Father! Bless us and all You have given us. Bless our friends and family . . . and send Your angels to deliver Your very many spiritual blessings lavished upon us in heavenly places, so they can be embedded deeply into our lives—so we are enriched in equal measure in the physical as we are in the spirit. Bless us till we are convinced of Your love, precious Father.   Amen.

CHAPTER THIRTY-SIX

CASTING

OUR CHOOSING FULFILS A GLORIOUS
PURPOSE TO FILL THE PLACE LUCIFER
ONCE HELD AND SUBSEQUENTLY LOST.

As Christians, we easily identify with Esther and her leading role in the kingdom. She too comes from nothing but finds herself swept up in the purposes of God until her life is full of privilege and significance.

Esther was just an orphan from a refugee family and yet in the end, her position and place became pivotal to the purposes of God and His people.

Esther's tale is our own.

We relate to her because we care about our destiny; those words, "For such a time as this," have us nodding in agreement even as they challenge our hearts and minds.

We know we are here for a reason. For us to play our part in the plans of God we will, like Esther, need a whole other level of courage and resolve.

That is straightforward. But what about the other characters?

Whom would we cast in the other roles? Who plays King Xerxes, Queen Vashti, Mordecai, and Haman? Wouldn't it be helpful to map the whole narrative into our story and situation? There is a richer perspective here to inform our context and environment, one that will inspire us to rise in courage to meet our moment of destiny in a similar way—surrounded by a full cast.

Esther 2:5-7

Haman and Mordecai . . .

Haman is the bad-guy. He was frustrated with Mordecai, his nemesis, as day after day he refused to bow to him. Riled and unable to tolerate this affront to his pride anymore, he set up gallows—an instrument of torture, humiliation and death to end him.

The wooden pole is easy to associate with the cross of Christ in our minds. In His temptation, Jesus refused to bow down to or submit to Satan; soon enough he makes and executes plans to be rid of Him and Jesus is led away to die.

It is clear as crystal—Jesus should be cast in Mordechai's role and Satan should fill Haman's.

For both Haman and Satan there was an unexpected twist in the tale as their expected victories suddenly backfired. In both cases the wooden gallows they have set up are used against them. Satan's power is destroyed at the Cross and Haman eventually dies on his own gallows. Both times the villain succumbs and the hero wins!

There is a marvellous moment where King Xerxes is talking to Haman. He asks, "What should be done for the one the king delights to honour?" Haman, convinced he is the man the king refers to, suggests the royal horse and robe should be used, and a declaration of honour should be proclaimed in the streets over this esteemed person.

How crushing for his ego when the king commands him to honour Mordecai instead—the man he had in mind to kill.

We can only imagine, too, how much it riled Satan to see Jesus honoured as He entered Jerusalem atop a horse on what we call Palm Sunday. The palm branches and coats thrown down and the cries of acclamation must have provoked him to his core—Jesus was being honoured, even while the enemy was scheming to murder him.

Now, let's turn back to King Xerxes and Queen Vashti and explore their part in recounting this saga . . .

Esther 6-7 | John 12:12-15

There came a day when a glorious archangel thumbed his nose at Father God. This insult plunged the kingdom of heaven into uncertainty and civil war. Eventually Lucifer was cast out so that peace could be restored. It was a betrayal so hurtful to the Lord because Lucifer's treachery came out of an intimate relationship.

Here in the book of Esther those parts are retold in the lives of a king and queen as they governed a great and glorious empire. Vashti's name and description both speak to her glory and beauty. Vashti loses her position because she did not value her place and felt free to humiliate her husband the king. Scripture teaches marriage is for the earth and not for heaven, yet marriage was the only physical idea adequate to portray how close God the Father and Lucifer were before his fall in this retelling. His treachery cut deep!

Xerxes plays the part of the Father.

The separation of Xerxes and Vashti happens before Esther's time, but it serves as an important background to the her story. Importantly, Esther replaces Vashti. Perhaps we should humbly contemplate what it means that we too are chosen to accomplish a glorious purpose—to fill the place Lucifer once held and subsequently lost.

At the most elementary level, this is a wonderful summary of our destiny as redeemed and restored humankind. Think of the many and varied lives of men and women throughout history. Politics and war, love and hate, power and poverty are best understood as we consider this prehistoric vacancy in heaven's court, now filled by humanity!

We are sometimes glorious but just as often exactly the opposite.

The original occupant opposes all our progress as we, mostly oblivious to what motivates us, seek to possess what another lost.

In response, vindictive hatred steals away, kills and destroys any gains made— dark interventions ensure that if the villain can't have his place anymore, then no one will. Confused and perplexed, we experience a combination of privilege and opposition without natural awareness of what has gone before.

Rev 12:7 | Esther 1 | Esther 2:15-18 | John 10:10

So now we take a breath and consider what the story of Esther might teach us if we view itin the context of the glorious backstory of God. It is nearly too much to take in as two distinct pictures of ourselves resolve before our eyes—in the first, we are taking our place before the Father, and in the other we are interceding in the face of a terrible threat.

Isn't it such a joy to behold Jesus in His dignity and conviction, as He subtly facilitates our relationship with the Father and coaches us in our role as an intercessor?

Our engagement with intercession is deeply linked to our position before him. Intimacy with the King and a raft of royal privileges are ours. This frees us to focus on the kingdom and the needs of those we represent rather than ourselves. We have displaced another who was distracted and thus lost both place and purpose. This is no time to remain silent—no time to disengage. We are so blessed. We have all we could hope and dream of. Now is our time to rise.

Esther 4:13-14

Q1.   How does the glory of Mordechai inform your worship of Christ as you consider it in this moment?

Q2.   What does it mean to you to have been given Lucifer's position and place?

Q3.   Compare yourself with Vashti. What does this mean for you in terms of your role as an intercessor?

Prayer.

Lord. Find us faithful. We value the place and position You have provided. We are grateful You chose us as Your close companions, friends and lovers. We want to delight Your soul and please You in every way. Grace us so all we are and have, might become sufficient for our role far above our native station. Take poor refugee orphans and make us fit for Your palace and comfortable at Your side.   Amen.

CHAPTER THIRTY-SEVEN

SUCH A TIME AS THIS

WHY DOES IT HAVE TO FEEL LIKE, IN THIS MOMENT, XERXES IS MORE HER MONARCH THAN HER HUSBAND, LOVER OR FRIEND?

When Esther was most vulnerable, Mordechai rescued her and took her into his own family. That's a bit like salvation for us. Later she is prepared and purified, and finally she becomes the wife of the king. The analogy holds. From the moment we are saved, the Holy Spirit sanctifies us, as a preparation for us to come into intimacy with the Father.

King Xerxes is a rare picture of Father God. The story of Esther's selection and her entrance into the palace reflects our experience as we determine to come before him, accepted and blameless in His sight.

The harem beauticians are a type of the Holy Spirit. They get Esther ready. Her time in the harem completely changes every aspect of her look and lifestyle—Before she meets her king face to face, she is prepared, beautified and cleansed.

Even so, Mordechai had a further role. He remained vitally interested in her welfare throughout the selection process as she rose to her eventual place at Xerxes' side. So, Jesus is the one who brings us before the Father and He works to keep us there.

"No one comes to the Father except through him"

How did Mordecai facilitate her? First he dealt with her identity. He forbade her to reveal who she used to be. To ascend is to leave behind our past orphan and refugee status. We too must let go of what we were, in order to take up our place. We need to leave our latent obsession with truth-telling which so hinders our intimacy with the Father. Christ calls us to discretion with respect to our past—and to do so prepares us to find favour in the Father's eyes.

This is like one of those TV shows when contestants are given a makeover and a new hairdo resulting in a complete transformation that leaves even family members stunned. But there is one thing more. The makeover is only complete when Esther leaves her old identity behind as well.

For us, this prelude to our assent into royalty is vital to understand. Once we were slaves and orphans, but now we have come to be accepted into intimate relationship with the Father, accepted as blameless before him.

You can imagine Esther's surprise as she became the one the emperor desired and selected. Her life became entirely different. King Xerxes gave her the position and place of the original queen, Vashti—including her entire estates. Similarly, we receive more than anticipated. Father God's intimate companions receive as an inheritance the place and position Lucifer lost—intimacy and authority follow each other closely in His mind and heart.

Time passed for the new queen.

Then later, the relationship between Esther and Xerxes was strained. In some way, this was so much so, that when an emergency arose in which Esther needed help, she did not feel close enough to her him to ask for help. No explanation was given for the distance between them and the apparent lack of intimacy. Unfortunately, her only access to the king was the way common to all his subjects. And that posed a problem—to come to him without an invitation threatened her life.

She found herself with no other option. When Haman threatened the future of the Jewish people, her people. It was up to the new queen to bring this matter before the king. Why did it have to feel like Xerxes was more her monarch than her husband, lover or friend? What could she do?

Yes, we know the story. She rose.

Gal 4:7 | Eph 1:3-6 | Esther 1:19 | Esther 4-5

In spite of her fears, she determined to act boldly!

Mordecai was right—was this not her destiny? She was born for this hour; still, this knowledge did little to calm her raging pulse as she approached the throne. Esther had no invitation, and to draw near without one breached kingdom protocol.

She risked it all to intercede for her people.

As we compare her situation with ours, we must consider the difference between convenient enjoyment of God's presence and engagement with the Father in the role of intercessor, even when it is feels inopportune, uncomfortable and inappropriate. Neither King Xerxes nor Father God are taken aback by a surprise visit. They both raise their hand in welcome.

In this posture of intercession, Esther now identified with her people. She took the opposite approach to the one she adopted early on in her relationship with the king. Both times she followed Mordechai's advice. When it was just about her and the king, her past identity was irrelevant.

But suddenly her origins became all important. It was the real key to the breakthrough required for her people—as her identification with her past empowered her purpose. The king took the plight of her people personally, because she was his and the problem was hers. Daniel chapter nine is a well-known demonstration of the same idea—intercession through identification:

> *And I prayed to the Lord my God, and made confession, and said, "O Lord, great and awesome God, who keeps His covenant and mercy with those who love Him, and with those who keep His commandments, we have sinned and committed iniquity, we have done wickedly and rebelled, even by departing from Your precepts and Your judgments. Neither have we heeded Your servants the prophets, who spoke in Your name to our kings and our princes, to our fathers and all the people of the land.*

One of my favourite parts of Esther's story is how she faced her fears and moved forward regardless.

Esther 4:10-12 | Esther 5:2 | Eph 1-2 | Esther 2:10 | Esther 7:3-4 | Dan 9:4-6

Haman was powerful, and no doubt well known to her already as a master manipulator of court politics, so she took her time to get to the point. She invited them both—Xerxes and Haman—to one party and then another until she finally managed to get her message across.

At her word, Haman was finished for good. Her authority with Xerxes was enough to obtain a great deliverance for her people—something significant to learn, for her and also for us.

As we intercede against unspeakable evil, hesitant steps still count, and the ultimate end of darkness is sure. Thankfully, it is inevitable that we will eventually prevail. When we realise we have such authority, we can face the battles and contend to shape the culture and the climate of our age.

It is not the strength of the enemy but our relationship with the Father that determines the outcome. The Bible says that Haman became terrified before the king and queen. In intercession, as we bring the accusation back on the accuser's head and reveal the real intentions of the evil one before the Father, he is terrified. In that moment, he knows he is finished.

Together we can stand against any evil and it will tremble in fear!

Haman dies. Queen Esther gets Haman's estates. Consider the thought—she has already taken Vashti's place, position and her estates. Now she receives Haman's lands as well. Satan is the name for Lucifer in his fallen form. Now we understand the root of his malevolence toward us—by taking our place in the heavenlies in Christ, we dispossessed the enemy once. Now, through intercession we take the dispossession one step further and deny his claim to this world as well.

Esther 5:4 | Esther 7:1-8:2

Q1.   What is in your hands now you have dispossessed Lucifer, just as Esther dispossessed Vashti?

Q2.   What is in your hands now Satan's estates have also been given to you, just as Haman's possessions were delivered over to Esther?

Q3.   What practical steps would you use to appoint Christ over Satan's estates, just as Esther handed Mordechai Haman's estates?

Prayer.

Lord. We are overwhelmed by where we find ourselves and daunted by the one whose estates, place and position we have inherited. Thank You for Christ, who is always at our side, always faithful and wise. Help us to move in a lifestyle of humility— continually determined to place all we contend for under His rule and reign. Let our lives be thank offerings, a savour received in heaven to glorify him.   Amen.

CHAPTER THIRTY-EIGHT

AN ENDURING LEGACY

THIS PLACES A KEY IN THE LOCK FOR US IN OUR
UNDERSTANDING OF THE LAW AND ITS EFFECT
ON OUR EVERYDAY LIVES.

Jesus will reign until every enemy is under His feet. Satan was conquered at the cross, but there is more to be done.

Esther knew that Haman's selfish conniving remained a threat until not only he, but his ten sons as well, were dead. And so she seeks permission from King Xerxes to impale the sons on the gallows with their father. Only then is the security and prosperity of her people assured—both in the moment, and for the years to come.

In spiritual warfare, we intercede and wrestle against principalities and powers and rulers in heavenly places. When we prevail, it is right and proper to honour the Hero by aligning all we have accomplished with His triumph at the cross.

> *He has made alive together with Him, having forgiven you all trespasses,*
> *having wiped out the handwriting of requirements that was against us,*
> *which was contrary to us. And He has taken it out of the way, having nailed*
> *it to the cross. Having disarmed principalities and powers, He made a public*
> *spectacle of them, triumphing over them in it.*

Even after Haman was dead and defeated, there was much to do. First his sons needed to go. Then the edict that threatened the lives and possessions of the Jewish people needed to be addressed.

Villains like to build monuments . . . to themselves. Before Absalom dies, he takes a pillar and sets it up as a monument to himself. Similarly, before Haman dies on the gallows, he arranges the institution of an irrevocable law that outlasts him.

Satan lost all his power at the cross, and yet a monument to his past influence remains in the form of law. In Christ, we know our relationship to the law has changed, so that it is fundamentally different to what the Old Testament people of God—those who lived before the cross—experienced, yet the law itself continues to endure into this new era, unheeding of the change.

We Christians easily get confused over two different paradigms in play at the same time. After all, we are aware of Jesus' words in Matthew:

> *For assuredly, I say to you, till heaven and earth pass away, one jot or one*
> *tittle will by no means pass from the law till all is fulfilled.*

This is easy to misunderstand. It is easy to believe the persistent nature of the law means we must remain subject to it for as long as it endures. However, the portrayal of a second law in tension with the first in the book of Esther provides a key to understanding our relationship with the law and with liberty in our everyday lives.

The first immutable edict is comparable with the Mosaic law. Its very nature is a persistent threat to the people of God. Its outcome is profoundly negative:

> *And the letters were sent by couriers into all the king's provinces, to*
> *destroy, to kill, and to annihilate all the Jews, both young and old, little*
> *children and women, in one day, on the thirteenth day of the twelfth month,*
> *which is the month of Adar, and to plunder their possessions.*

The law condemns us. It brings us nothing but pain while we are under it. The Jewish people in the story were to be killed, annihilated and plundered. It is easy to identify these as the work of the one who comes to steal, kill and destroy.

Who knew?

The Law was God-given, written by the finger of God,

> but indirectly, it has Satan's fingerprints all over it.

2 Sam 18:18 | Esther 3:5-12 | Matt 5:18 | Esther 3:13

Ultimately, the Jews found deliverance by rallying around a different edict, a rule not designed to annul the first one, but to contend against the original law's effectiveness. The new law came from Mordecai just as . . . "grace and truth came by Jesus Christ," circumventing the "law of sin and death."

Mordecai possesses authority to mandate a new law. It is the same authority Haman used to initiate the first one.

Xerxes repossesses his signet ring from Haman after his death, and gives it to Mordecai instead. The signet ring speaks of delegated authority to act on behalf of the king and advise him.

The king, fully aware of the implications, accepts Mordechai's new law. It opposes the effect of the original law and annuls its power, even though the first law remains. The same is true for us. There are two laws in play.

> *There is therefore now no condemnation to those who are in Christ Jesus,*
> *who do not walk according to the flesh, but according to the Spirit. For the*
> *law of the Spirit of life in Christ Jesus has made me free from the law of sin and death.*

As we follow the narrative, the nature and purpose of the second edict are described:

> *By these letters the king permitted the Jews who were in every city to gather*
> *together and protect their lives—to destroy, kill, and annihilate all the forces*
> *of any people or province that would assault them, both little children and*
> *women, and to plunder their possessions.*

Empowered by the second law, the people rose up to defend themselves and their possessions against an attack of their enemies that had been licenced by the first law—and they triumphed repeatedly until peace arrived! Nothing was left of the wicked schemes of Haman. God's people prevailed as the second immutable law overcame the first.

There is a freshness here—a new way to view the law and also ourselves.

Isn't it so poignant and revealing to see the spirited tension between bondage and liberty for supremacy in the lives of God's people?

Exodus 31:18 | Rom 8:1-2 | Esther 8:2, 11

As we fight against Satan's apparently rock-solid schemes against us, we shift from being law-keepers, weighed down by condemnation and guilt, to enjoying the glorious freedom of the rule of Christ.

This could be transformational, but only if we rise up to defend ourselves.

Q1.   How does the second edict inform your view of law-keeping and enjoyment of the grace of God?

Q2.   What is the intention and natural outcome of the first edict for the people of God?

Q3.   Consider the legal ramifications of two edicts in play with one set to oppose the other. How is Christ's law of life a fight for you to receive? What do you think hinders you from receiving and appropriating Christ's law of the spirit of life?

Prayer.

Lord. We want to honour Christ and His role in our freedom from the law of sin and death. Thank you. We have a chance now, to live and love and find where we fit within Your purposes. Reach into our soul and plant a blazing courage there, so we are enabled to contend for the wellbeing of our loved ones, Your people and Your kingdom. Lead us to victory, Lord—Set Your people free from the awful tyranny of the one who has destined us for destruction and ruin.   Amen.

CHAPTER THIRTY-NINE

THE LAW OF CHRIST

THE CONSEQUENCES OF SATAN'S MEDDLING AT
THE FALL PUT GOD'S PEOPLE AT RISK.
SOMETHING NEEDED TO BE DONE.

At this point, you probably feel a little uncomfortable. Wasn't the law of Moses God-given? How can these two sacred stone tablets be associated with the villain?

The Mosaic law was given as a benevolent act of God. It helped God's people and kept them safe until Christ could come, in the way a governess or schoolmaster keeps children in their care, protected from danger.

Moses stood between two mountains. He cried out to the people that he was setting before them "blessings and cursing, life and death." It follows intuitively—the law had been given; from that point on, the world was fundamentally changed. After all, laws usually function this way. Parliament make laws. They are announced publicly. And usually, immediately thereafter, they are policed and enforced.

We expect the same thing in the giving of God's law, but on another level—aren't divine laws written, mandated and enforced from on high, in that order?

It makes sense, but I don't think so . . .

You see, death and the curse did not begin at Sinai. Yes, the law was new, but the cause and effect they revealed had been in play long before Moses brought them down the mountain to the Jewish people.

Gal 3:24 | Deut 1126-29 | Heb 12:18-24 | Rom 5:12

Actually, their revelation did not change the state of play for humanity on the planet in any way. Still, what happened was important—now the Jews could see what was going on.

They could perceive the way of death and the curse, and they could discern the pathway of blessing. No guarantees, but they could now see their way clear to attempt to walk in wisdom and righteousness.

The Mosaic law was a benevolent gift from God to His people. As they camped by Sinai they received a clear revelation designed to illuminate elementary forces—structures pre-existent and profound, completely hidden since creation millennia before.

The Lord shone a light on the inner workings of our world. Now the people of God had a clear advantage. While pagans groped around in the dark, wondering at the fickleness of their gods with their unpredictable moods and constantly dumbfounded by the ways their lives unfolded, the Jews had an edge over them.

David said it this way, "Your word is a lamp unto my feet and a light unto my path."

Lamp in hand, the Jewish people held all the cards!

The Mosaic law was revelatory rather than a creative act. In its essence it was redemptive and kind, and as such, it does not compare to the immutable law initiated by Haman in the story of Esther.

To find an exact point of comparison, we need to go further back in time.

Satan comes into Eden and corrupts creation. Sin, death and the curse, not present prior to this, enter as a result of the Fall. His meddling put God's people at risk—the invisible forces undergirding cause and effect in our world shifted from being centred on the shared joy of the eternal Father and Son, to reflecting the archaic tension between the Hero and the villain and their ultimate destinies. And with that, the curse took its place alongside the undiluted blessing God had intended for humanity.

Exod 19-33 | Gal 4:3, 9 | Col 2:8, 20 | Ps 119:105 | Rom 5:12-13 | Prov 4:18-19

Centuries on, God countered this move at Sinai, providing revelation—a lamp for their feet—to His chosen people. This assisted them to navigate a corrupted world (it also introduced accountability in light of that revelation—not our focus here). Paul in Romans says it this way:

> *Therefore, just as through one man sin entered the world, and death through sin, and thus death spread to all men, because all sinned . . . until the law sin was in the world . . . death reigned from Adam to Moses . . .*

Paul, in his letters to both the Colossian and Galatian Christians, references elemental or fundamental forces. He strongly encourages them and us to not submit to them. He clearly had in mind the Mosaic law and the unseen forces within creation behind the scenes, reflected by that law.

His audience's position in Christ was pivotal to what he had to say. In Christ, it is no longer appropriate to live our lives desperately trying to stay on-script. In Him we are free from Haman's edict because we subvert the destroyer, the murderer and the plunderer thanks to Mordechai's law. The story of the Hero and the villain shapes the landscape of the world on which we plant our feet, but the Hero Himself has caught us up to live each day in a position elevated above these primitive dynamics.

To put ourselves under those forces or the law that makes them visible puts us back in the hands of the one responsible for corruption of God's plan for blessing in this world—we end up living out the will and destiny of the villain on his script rather than honouring and following the Hero into His glory.

We were orphans who knew no other reality than the slave-driver's cruel whip. We were filled with fear and dread—no future or relief in sight. But Christ, our hero came and lived among us. He was a wonderful anomaly! Unbowed, He bore the lash. No hardship common to us could break His spirit. He lifted up our heads and our hearts and spoke of another way. He gave us permission to resist.

We find ourselves in a fight for our lives. We rebel every day, determined to conquer, contend and prevail.

Rom 5:12-14 | Gal 4:3, 9 | Col 2:8, 20

Then the Hero leads us into an elevated position and place with intercessory influence over creation and even the scripts themselves. Seated with Him in heavenly places, we look down to where angels administer justice in line with the scripts, delivering blessing or cursing as appropriate.

We share a place with the Hero, the King of the Angel Armies.

Intimacy and intercession, purpose and position—we cannot enjoy all our privileges without putting them on the line as we live out our purpose. Moreover, the effectiveness of our intercessory work, enabled by our intimate access to Father God, is fundamentally connected to the law of the spirit of life in Christ Jesus so that we can be agents of blessing, healing and freedom wherever we go.

We bind up wounds. We loose the captives. We dispense grace. We reverse destinies. We lift up heads and hearts and restore the fortunes of the oppressed!

Just as Christ came not to judge but to save us from ourselves and the consequences of our foolish and rebellious choices, we also resist the temptation to judge and instead chose to release blessing in and over the lives of all, even those who deserve the opposite.

In rising above, we subvert the natural outcomes of the law and the invisible forces embedded within our corrupted creation, annulling their threat in our own lives and the lives around us. Walking in confidence, authority and faith, we take our place in all that is now true of us in Christ. And the world will never be the same!

Eph 2:4-7 | John 3:17 | John 12:47 | Matt 18:18

Q1.   How is your life simultaneously a time of battle, of victory and also of celebration?

Q2.   Each year since, Jews have a celebration called Purim to remember this victory. What regular celebration of grace has a place in your life? How could you embed a point of remembrance celebration into your family culture centred on the wonder of Christ bringing us under His law of life?

Q3.   As the Passover is to Communion, Purim is to . . . ?

Prayer.

Lord. Christ we celebrate You as the author of life. Quicken us according to Your word, by aligning our thoughts and actions to Your law of life. Strengthen us. We would fight well for grace and redemption in the lives of those You have given us. Search us and know us and lead us in the way everlasting, for our victory rests on Your righteousness and within Your ways. Lead us on strongly.   Amen.

CHAPTER FORTY

TWO CHOICES

A STORY OF GLORY INTERRUPTED BY
OBEDIENCE TO DEATH AND GREAT LOSS. TO
STAY ON-SCRIPT, TAKE A LOOK AT JESUS.

Many down through the centuries have chosen to play the part of the villain, and as they embraced their role, everything around them hurried them toward disgrace, rejection, ridicule, loss and eventually, humiliation and death.

Until the time of Christ, this was the very definition of folly. Wisdom was found in the opposite direction—the fear of the Lord was the beginning of wisdom. Aligning our life with the character of God and this ancient story of God opened up the possibility of a blessed life.

When Christ came, however, He voluntarily embraced the curse and its consequences so that we who embrace Him could be free from the law of sin and death, and this opened the way to blessing for us.

He chose to play the part of the villain, right up to the point where He reached the final destination.

Paul says that if we do the same things and get the same results, we have no excuse. Redemption or ruin, the choice comes to us all. When Christ chose the villain script and its predictable consequences, He chose ruin! He was strung up in disgrace—a public spectacle—his agony, humiliation and apparent waste of a life serving only as a warning to others, until He finally died.

Prov 9 | John 10:17-18 | Gal 3:13 | Rom 1:20

He also chose the hero script. In His life, rather than His death, scripture is adamant that He fulfilled the law in its entirety. His life was exactly on script! When He was playing the hero He was on point, and the way He lived and the choices He made were entirely and absolutely glorifying to God.

For me this has become a barometer of what a God-glorifying life is all about. God is most glorified when we are most Christ-like. When I say that I mean that we are conformed to the image of His son, and when I say *that* I am focussed on Him in the primeval past rather than in His incarnation.

So when Christ took on flesh and played the hero, He glorified God. And when He had perfectly pulled that off in only half a lifetime, He pivoted to the end of the villain script, so that He could get that over and done with, once and for all, so no one ever needs to live under the threat of a ruined life!

Christ the man is not the reference point. Instead He referenced His own tale and identity from way back and leveraged all of the dynamics that relied so heavily on His backstory, to open up heroism for us all.

The incarnate Christ brought about the redemption of humanity and indeed the entire world through His shrewd expertise in wielding the power of the scripts.

In ages past, the scribes of heaven wrote of the Hero's deeds and their words on the page defined the hero script. Back then, Christ authored an ideal. In His incarnation He perfected what it meant to live a life on-script, in line with His heroic deeds of old. He is both the "author and perfecter" of our faith, and the one we should fix our eyes on as we ourselves journey forward. Philippians chapter two holds Him up as an exemplary on-script life. If you want to stay on-script, take a look at Jesus.

It encourages us to share the same mind as the one who overcame by emptying Himself and stooped low prior to a final exaltation.

His life retells an epic tale with a pure and undiminished clarity . . .

If this is the best chance we will ever possess to glimpse the story of the Son in His existence before time began, it comes as a surprise—as a story of glory

Matt 5:17 | Heb 12:2 | Phil 2:5-11

interrupted by obedience to death and great loss—but in the end there is guaranteed exaltation.

Christ stoops and descends into ambiguity. He has the same identity but clothes Himself in fleshly rags. As He is rejected by the leadership of the day and even His family, He plays the Hero in His original humiliation. As He falls from grace, and as His life ebbs away, He temporarily plays the villain. As He rises into glory and triumph, He is Himself again. As He is finally vindicated, His story rises to higher levels of wonder, majesty and glory.

In the end, father and son will stand together victorious and full of joy in their united bond and final magnificence.

Through it all He was and always will be, the Hero Himself.

Isa 53:8-9

Q1.   How can you be more on-script? How can you be more Christ-like in this regard?

Q2.   Try to articulate what Christ shared about Himself on the Emmaus Road?

Q3.   So what? What are the ramification to your perspective and life if the reference point for righteousness and blessing is not Christ in His incarnate life, but rather His life and deeds at a time prior to creation?

Prayer.

Lord. We value Christ in this moment as we see the extremes He went to bless and save us. He was despised, and we did not esteem Him - Surely He carried our sorrows. We shout "Worthy," and bow the knee to the one who made His place with the wicked, aligning His fortunes with the villain, so our destinies might be bathed in hope and the affirmation of the Father's heart. Help us dear Saviour to make much of Your sacrifice. Amen.

CHAPTER FORTY-ONE

SAFETY IN THE

_____

DANIEL SAW ANOTHER SUNRISE, ABRAHAM RETURNED HOME WITH HIS SON, AND DAVID TOOK UP HIS KINGDOM AGAIN.

The cataclysm brought on by Lucifer's betrayal and subsequent revolt was extreme. In David's life, this aspect of the original tale seems underplayed, but we have other places to turn to see the enormity of it's impact. Where do we see an impressive start and then loss and calamity, and then a rise to greater heights?

Of course, we cannot go past Job as a poignant illustration of this.

He was an amazing man, a friend of God and blameless in his lifestyle. Blamelessness is no small thing. Instead of brokenness and woundedness— Satan struggles to find a way in. Job had a lack of buttons to push and strings to pull. He is fallible, but it is a little like when Jesus says, "The enemy is coming and he has nothing in Me to work with." Job was wealthy, blessed and generous, and that bothered the Devil more than we can imagine.

Then disaster came, and in a single day one thing after another went wrong. Suddenly his children were dead, and his wealth and health gone. He was fine one minute and suddenly nothing was left!

Let's take this following summary as a working definition of the original hero script:

The original script of Father God's life played out in the following way— Things were coming together. There was accomplishment and glory. Then there is a point

of difficulty, pain and loss. Following this, there is a long rebuilding
towards even greater honour, glory and strength.

Jesus emptied Himself and then was highly exalted. Job becomes empty too, experiencing so much loss it seems unbearable! Aligned to the heroic pattern, by the end of the book, he came back stronger than ever, and the Bible is very clear—his eventual position was greater and more prosperous than what he enjoyed before the calamity came. He suffered the loss of all things and then rose to a position greater than his former state.

His life followed the script, and we all look on compelled. We sense a sacred aspect to his tale—a glimpse into unseen and unheard mysteries. His life exemplifies and reflects the deepest dynamics of our world and the humility and subsequent vindication of the pre-existent Son of God.

Mount Moriah for Abraham was another variation of this archetype. His world was centred on the life of his son. If Isaac were to die, that would cause Abraham to suffer the loss of all things. Irrespective, when God instructs him to go to the mountain and slay his son, he obeys. There was a lot going on. However, the enormity of his obedience-act triggers a change in the spiritual status of the patriarch. "Now I can bless you!" God says. As he obediently and humbly embraced loss, he moved forward to a significant milestone on the hero script. Now the blessing on his life could rise to a level he had never before attained.

Job's loss, the incarnation and death of Jesus, Mt Moriah, David's exile, and Daniel in the lion's den are all retellings of the story of Father God.

Folks in trouble often look up and shake a fist at the heavens as it were. "Why me?" they cry. "Don't You care?"

We never knew . . .

We had no idea how empathetic the heart of the Father must be during these kind of episodes in our lives. He suffered the loss of all things. He knows how it feels.

He has been there.

Job 42:12-17 | Phil 3:8 | Gen 22:17-18

God is not the author of evil in our lives, but He too has been touched by the full extent of pain and loss.

Why don't we sit beside David as he mourns the demise of a rebellious son, sobbing in heartbreak? Why don't we sit in the ashes in sackcloth with Job awhile or climb to the heights of Moriah and wrestle with potential heartbreak alongside Abraham, the ancient patriarch? As we do, and as we linger with these men in their darkest days, we begin to know God the Father better as they retell His story in all its pathos.

In the deep depressing slump and as the pieces of our lives fall down upon us—there is safety there. The power of the script is so great it guaranteed the subsequent reconstruction and glory phases. It allows us to say, though I have fallen, yet will I rise! True to the script, Job got his life back with interest, Abraham came home with his son, and David returned to Jerusalem to take up his kingdom and throne again.

Catastrophe does not guarantee eventual vindication but an on-script stance in the face of disaster ties our story to the epic tale of Father God's ultimate comeback story. In like manner, we are carried through and beyond the impact of the threat at hand . . . towards greater glory.

Father God and Lucifer both have declines in their storyline. One is a low and painful doorway followed by an ascent from glory into more glory. The other is a descent from which there is no return.

James 1:13-17 | 2 Sam 18:33-19:8 | Job 2:8 | Gen 22 | Micah 7:8 | Job 42:12-17
Gen 22:19 | 2 Sam 19:9-20:3

Q1.   Why does God allow us to suffer? Where does it come from, if not God's direct action?

Q2.   Does God care when you go through difficult times?

Q3.   Have negative times ever borne fruit in your life? What do you think of hard times as a source of safety?

Prayer.

Lord. We have had enough trite answers to life's deep and difficult questions. We want to grapple, to contend, to wrestle with who You are and what each days brings. We desire the fellowship of Your sufferings to align us with Your choices and Your priorities. We chose the humble path—the narrow road to life. We determine to hold on till morning, so as to rest easy in Your image at daybreak. Our will is insufficient for these things but our desire for You draws us on to find You in every and any moment of our lives. Hold us in a place of safety as we bear the whirlwind and fire, and privilege us to look beyond and see the face of God.   Amen.

CHAPTER FORTY-TWO

SHIP OF FOOLS

IN EVERY TRIBE AND TOWN, VILLAGE AND CITY
THERE ARE RUINED LIVES, REGARDLESS OF
BACKGROUND, CLASS OR RACE.

In the early chapters of Romans, Paul lays out two pathways or realities. One leads to life and peace and the other promises certain peril. This context frames his famous unpacking of the meaning of faith, grace and Gospel. Yes, we have heard something like that before, when Moses said, "I set before you either life and death. Choose life!"

We live in a world of both blessing and curse. The character of God is written into His creation through the scripts, just as any artist leaves their distinctive and recognisable mark upon their work. The fingerprints of God on His creation ensure it opposes the wicked and favours the righteous.

I guess if someone wakes up one morning feeling as though the whole world is against him or her, they may well be correct.

The billionaire and the beggar both feel its touch, but usually everyday situations are so complicated it is unwise to look at people's circumstances and draw direct conclusions about this sort of thing. Jesus Himself discouraged judgement of people on this basis.

We need to be aware of these forces for a different reason—a redemptive purpose rather than a judgemental one!

Rom 2:7-11 | Deut 30:15-20 | Prov 3:34 | James 4:6 | 1 Peter 5:5 | John 9:3

We are placed in a similar context to Jesus in His incarnation. People all around are subject to the elemental forces of the hero and villain scripts—they are carried to their natural conclusions, towards blessing or ruin.

We come with a knowledge of the invisible landscape in order to save rather than to condemn. We are to be an opposing force, intervening to save the world from itself and the forces that drag it under.

The truth is that humanity already has Haman's edict. They already have the elemental forces. They already have the law to condemn them.

Romans teaches along similar lines. Pagans (non-Jews) have little idea of the landscape, but the Jews have an advantage over the pagan. Their Mosaic law illuminates these forces to the Jew. They see and understand the cause and effect behind the blessings and curses. They have the advantage of a perspective that discerns the difference between wisdom and foolishness.

The forces are a permanent part of the make-up of creation, the reason Jesus says:

> *For assuredly, I say to you, till heaven and earth pass away, one jot or one tittle will by no means pass from the law till all is fulfilled.*

The forces and creation are woven together so they will both endure until they are destroyed together.

When Paul writes a letter to the early church in Rome he discusses the slippery slope. He vividly describes a lifestyle shaped around the villain script like this:

> *For since the creation of the world His invisible attributes are clearly seen, being understood by the things that are made, even His eternal power and Godhead, so that they are without excuse.*

He did not intend to indicate a lack of excuse based on everyone in the world's easy access to the beauty of creation, and therefore an opportunity to recognise the creator's handiwork or character. Yes, the essence of His story is engraved within every aspect of creation, but no, that is not the logic of his argument even though it is a common view.

Gal 4:3, 9 ⏐ Col 2:8, 20 ⏐ John 3:17 ⏐ John 12:47 ⏐ Rom 2 ⏐ Ps 119:105 ⏐ Matt 5:18 Rom 1:20

Instead, he points out that everyone in the world has front row seats from which to view demonstrations of the curse and its consequences at work. He suggests we should recognise these forces' existence as an evidence of the Maker's mark.

The forces act to benefit those who share the Maker's character and the narrative of His life—the hero script. They resist those in opposition to His ways—those who prefer to live out the script of the original villain instead.

This becomes clear as we read on:

> . . . although they knew God, they did not glorify Him as God, nor were thankful, but became futile in their thoughts, and their foolish hearts were darkened. Professing to be wise, they became fools . . . And even as they did not like to retain God in their knowledge, God gave them over to a debased mind, to do those things which are not fitting; being filled with all unrighteousness, sexual immorality, wickedness . . . who, knowing the righteous judgment of God, that those who practice such things are deserving of death, not only do the same but also approve of those who practice them.

Not everyone in this world has the privilege of a life filled with the unspoilt beauty of creation. Slavery, depravation, trafficking, war and famine all conspire to hide it from millions every day. The beauty of creation is not the proof that leaves an entire world without excuse. No, instead, the curse at work teaches that particular truth to us all. It teaches a lesson that every soul on this planet may learn.

Bad choices result in eventual ruin—isolation, pain and ridicule. Train-wrecked lives teach an awesome truth, that there is a Creator and He favours righteousness, faithfulness and humility. His character, written into the fabric of this world opposes unrighteousness, faithlessness and pride.

In every tribe and town, village and city inevitably there are ruined lives.

The prodigal, the village-idiot, the bum, the kid lost in a smoky haze of drug use. Silver spoon or not. Good-living family or not. The principle remains—a lifestyle of choices in opposition to the character of God leads to ruin. You don't need to

Rom 1:21-32

go far to see it either in New York or in Calcutta. In an African tribe or the Amazon, it is the same—there is universal evidence to hint at something subtle going on behind the scenes.

People who sit in the gutter at the bottom of the slippery slope are a global reality. The world looks on, as they become a huge billboard with a single message.

When wel, as humanity, make idiot choices, then bad things happen.

Intuitively one leads to the other, and yet so often we presume the negative consequences involved are the result of God's direct intervention.

Yes, God opposes the proud, but not directly. He created the world we live in and shaped it to bless those with similar preferences. Then came the fall and creation's corruption, just a few days into the history of the world apparently, and from there both the hero and the villain scripts came into play with their associated blessings and curses.

With this then as a legal basis, angels administer justice in this world, and demons tempt and accuse.

As we stand back and look again with all of this in view, we see God taking credit for *indirect* action. He even warns of consequences, perhaps with words like, "I will judge you according to your ways," even though such judgement is simply a result of the natural cause and effect of the way the world is wired.

The more I have considered these things, the more I have become convinced that God does not *actively* punish humanity. Judgement was not His intent in His creative work. Neither is it His objective now. Perhaps the Book of Jonah taken as a whole articulates this dynamic best, even assisting us to grapple with our own response to God's unexpected actions and attitudes in the context of deserved judgement.

Instead, He is redemptive to the very core. He intervenes to hold back judgement because it is out of step with His mind and heart for humanity.

As I read scripture with that context in mind, more often than not I see the hand of God opposed to these consequences and set to resist the forces empowered by the hero and villain scripts, even though it is His backstory that they retell.

Ezek 7:3 | Jonah

Return with me to Romans chapter one for a moment. Watch as we find the hand of God, not pushing us over the brink of the slippery slope, but rather holding onto us all as long as possible. For some who go too far, He eventually lets go. They are handed over or given up to receive their just deserts. However, His gracious intervention in opposition to the scripts' power allows some to realise their mistake before it is too late and to take hold of His hand while His grasp on them remains. The kindness of God leads to repentance, and mercy triumphs over judgement.

As we reflect, we notice the villain script repeating. One generation after another looks on and regardless of the consequences they see in the lives of those around them, they walk the same path. They plummet down a horrific downward spiral of despair. They approve of their foolish heroes and follow suit. What motivates them to self-harm of this nature? I wonder, would it be going too far, or would it be out of place, to refer to the curse as contagious?

Rom 1:26a | Rom 2:4 | James 2:13 | Rom 1:32

Q1.   If the curse and ruin is contagious, if is fair enough to fear for those who lead "lawless" lives? What should be our response? How can this fear draw us into legalism?

Q2.   If God actively engages to resist the just consequences of our actions, what or who is repsonsible for the punishment of poor behaviour?

Q3.   If law-keeping only treats the symptoms of the horrible and deadly disease with its detrimental pull on so many lives, how should it be treated— with a view to acting on the cause or real root of the problem?

Prayer.

Lord. We stand beside You in Your grief and love, as You see so many fall prey to ruin. We want to be part of Your redemptive purposes, so we wait on You to teach us Your ways. Keep us from falling ourselves. Hold us in Your hand. Keep us from villainy and disgrace. Make us into Your hands and feet, graced with generosity of spirit, and a will to pluck those who suffer under the weight of their foolish choices from the road to pedition and all of its consequences.   Amen.

CHAPTER FORTY-THREE

CONTAGIOUS CURSE

EVERYONE IS SEEKING FOLLOWERS AND A
LOT OF THEM, PSALM ONE WOULD
ENCOURAGE US TO UNFOLLOW AS QUICKLY
AS POSSIBLE.

In our church, we often say, "When you choose your friends, you choose your future."

As parents, it's easy to find ourselves full of worry about the company our children keep. Peer pressure, especially in the age of social media, can be unrelenting. Why do we find it such a big deal? Jesus seemed to be Teflon coated. We find Him so often alongside those who were off script, and it does not seem to drag Him down at all. Should we follow His lead without fear? What about our children and loved ones?

Is the curse contagious or not?

Up to this point in the book, most of our observations relate to an Old Testament context and mindset—a reflection of the highest aspects of wisdom in this world whether expressed by academic professors or philosophers, religious scholars, psychiatrists or life coaches.

This chapter especially, is not to be understood as representing a New Covenant point-of-view either. For now, let's content ourselves with an answer to the question from a natural perspective. So . . .

Yes, the curse *is* contagious, and we have every reason to worry!

This very fact warrants fear in our hearts and causes us to reach for law and impose it on our love ones. Our minds fill with worry and our mouths sound warnings.

It's okay! Later we will find Jesus, receive the Holy Spirit and breathe a sigh of relief, but for now, worry is appropriate.

Why don't we begin in the very first verse of the Book of Psalms?

> *Blessed is the man who walks not in the counsel of the ungodly, nor stands in the path of sinners, nor sits in the seat of the scornful.*

Blessing is dependent on the company you keep. To loiter with those on the wrong road positions you on the same path. The psalm goes on to make the two destinations clear. If the curse were not contagious, there would be no need for sentiment of this kind. It is an endorsement for quarantine or isolationism, for sure. It was for this very reason Israel was not to intermarry with foreigners in the Promised Land.

In terms of natural consequences, poor outcomes are often caused by bad influences. A better perspective, however, would be to understand our world in terms of *unseen* cause and effect.

The Canaanites, the original people of the land had followed the cursed path to the point where consequently, their irrecoverable fall was imminent. They were to lose their place and their inheritance and they were to experience dispossession.

> *Then He said to Abram: "Know certainly that your descendants will be strangers in a land that is not theirs, and will serve them, and they will afflict them . . . but in the fourth generation they shall return here, for the iniquity of the Amorites is not yet complete."*

By the time the children of Israel entered the Promised Land the Canaanite's iniquity had reached its full measure. A spiritual bond through marriage would spiritually pollute future generations. It would threaten their inheritance. Instead of the hidden forces of the hero script at work to miraculously support their futures, villainy would be in play, society would disintegrate, and the promises of God would be at risk.

"Hang on. That is a good description of exactly what happened in the book of Judges. Tolerance bred a culture among the people of God identical to what they were there to displace and replace, and everything went to the dogs!"

Ps 1:1 | Gen 15:13-16

The bond did not need to be a strong one for the relationship to pass on the contagious curse. "Don't walk with them, stand with them or sit around to chat with them," the psalm says.

The curse was contagious and an antidote was required.

Galatians describes the law as a tutor, schoolmaster or guardian. Its job was to keep God's people safe until Christ came. He would come with a superior approach sufficient to deal fully with all of this toxicity.

The law kept the contagion at bay . . . temporarily.

If we accept this dynamic, it gives us some perspective on a few parts of the Mosaic Law we often find difficult to digest. Why was the rebellious son eventually put to death if he didn't reconsider his lifestyle? In fact, why was the death penalty applied for *so many* indiscretions? The reason was that Christ had not yet come with the cure, so when people chose the path of the villain, and their course was set past the point of return, their removal from society was the only way to stem the tide of the corruption.

I have Romans in mind again as I write: "If you do the same things and end up in the same devastating mess, you have no excuse."

The train-wrecked lives of the wicked should be a warning to us all. Naturally speaking, they should give us pause and cause us to keep our distance.

This brings me to a related subject.

There is an tremendous lot of "following" nowadays.

One click and you are connected . . . Everyone out there in cyberspace is after followers. But the first Psalm would encourage us to unfollow many of them as quickly as possible. *Do not linger with them. Do not friend them. Do not follow them. You do not want what is on them to tarnish your spiritual inheritance and drag you down.*

Here is the point.

Following another person activates powerful, unseen and unexpected forces.

Gal 3:23-25 | Deut 21:18-21 | Ps 1:1

You can only be on one script or the other, and when you associate with those who, aware or not, follow the original villain and retell his story, you follow them and him to their final destination—ruin, destruction and death.

The 'follow' is like the party game where a bunch of people parade around with their arms on the shoulders of the person in front. A train of people race forward, across time and down through the generations, until they eventually reach their natural and regrettable end.

In terms of the way the world is wired, it is true . . .

    When you choose your friends, you choose your future!

    The curse is contagious.

    And a follow is stickier than we realised.

Q1.   Who do you follow? What do you predict the outcome will be?

Q2.   Look around at those you love. As you look on, how does the stickiness of who they follow affect them? How could you and how should you intervene?

Q3.   If following is as sticky and powerful as described, who would you chose to follow, and why?

Prayer.

Lord. Thank You for those who have acted as waypoints for our lives. Thank You for those who have exemplified righteousness and uprightness. We praise You for surrounding us over the years with those who cared and led in right directions. Make us those who stand apart as light in a world gone awry. Make us beacons of hope for those who have lost their way.   Amen.

CHAPTER FORTY-FOUR

INFECTIOUS BLESSING

IT IS AS IF WE INNATELY KNOW THAT
A CONNECTION WITH HIM WILL
PROPEL US FORWARD IN A SIMILAR
WAY.

There is a power here to either propel us forward or drag us down. Jesus said, "Follow me." So did Paul. In reference to Jesus' impeccable mastery of the original hero script, Paul suggests that we would do well to share the Saviour's mind and heart.

Just follow Jesus as He followed the script.

In our mind's eye, we see a train of people again, but this time their destination is in the direction of blessing!

It is there again when Paul writes to Timothy. He fixates on the relationship between the young leader and his mother and grandmother. Follow the leader, and keep the generational momentum in the right direction.

Many years ago, when I learned to ride a motorcycle, the instructor shared a trick with me. If I focussed my eyes on where I wanted to go, there was some kind of crazy magic at work, so that wherever I looked, for better or worse, I ended up going in that direction. It was a physical phenomenon. The 'follow' works much the same way—walk in step a while and suddenly you are gripped by the power of one script or the other and you will be sure to arrive at its destination!

Matt 16:24 | Matt 19:21 | Mark 1:17 | Phil 2:5 | 1 John 2:6 | 2 Tim 1:4-5

The concept of this book began in a moment in church when I reflected on our seemingly universal connection with King David. Even though we learn a lot from the apostles and their writings, and even though we all respect Abraham, the father of faith, David comes out on top, if we had to choose. Regardless of the respect we hold for all the bible greats—Miriam, Debra, Elijah, Nehemiah or Moses—none can compete with David for his place in our hearts.

We have a collective affinity for David.

Most if not all of us identify strongly with him.

Talking to some friends after that service, I realised I was hearing this on repeat.

So many people I had spoken to, regardless of their place in the pew or the pulpit, had a similar affinity for this particular man. Male or female, old or young, there was something special that drew us to David.

Is this the case for you too?

How much have you tracked with David on his life journey?

I realised that day, that something was going on, and I was determined to figure it out. So I got to work . . .

Two ideas came out of my initial research and study.

The first was a simple realisation—the kings who followed David were graded according to the extent to which they aligned their lives to his standard.

> They were either like him or not.
>
> No middle ground.
>
> God made him an exemplar and ideal—a calibration point for other people's lives, especially his descendants, the kings who came after him.

Secondly, I observed that there was an innate sense of expectation in our spirits—as we track with David and associate with him through his down days, we expect to also experience the more glorious outcomes of his later life.

2 Kings 16:2 | 2 Kings 22:1-2

It is as if we innately understand the idea of a life on script, but replace the original hero script with David's life script as our point of reference.

Through times where he wandered in the wilderness and was forced into exile and isolation—long years without appreciation or esteem—we connect out story with his. We follow him. Those parts of his life are entry points or on-ramps for us. It is as if we know that a connection with him in his humility as we patiently wait with him in the wings will propel us forward into better days, until we somehow share in his vindication.

The power of the script is precedent—history repeating itself. By the grace of God it is possible to align our lives to David's . . . or another hero of the faith. Every time we do this, we set ourselves up as a reference point and we make it easier for those who have lost their way in a world woefully lacking a true north.

It turns out that we do not have to connect with the original version of the hero script—any genuine retelling will do.

We can use David's, Christ's, or Paul's life to orient ourselves and enjoy the benefits of an on-script lifestyle. You could look to your mother, your grandfather, an elder in the church, or someone else who demonstrates a certain x-factor suggestive of the truth that they are firmly on-script—favoured, blessed and worth following.

The power of this simple dynamic is phenomenal.

The disciples follow Jesus at His invitation. The favour on His life was tangible. He was on script, and His life means so much to us, yet His incarnate life serves us further—it serves as our pattern and example, just as it was for the disciples.

In fact, we are encouraged to . . .

> [look] unto Jesus, the author and finisher of our faith . . .

He created the world and wrote the scripts into its fabric using His fingertips. As He came, He perfected the art of living on-script. You would expect everyone else would pale beside him, but surprisingly, when He spoke to His disciples

Hebrews 12:2

one day, He revealed another principle to guide our understanding of these things,

> *. . . he who believes in Me, the works that I do he will do also; and*
> *greater works than these . . .*

Those who come after amplify what has gone before.

Solomon superseded and surpassed David. Elisha did the same to Elijah. Not only is blessing and the curse contagious and transmitted by following a leader, each successive generation receives a magnified dose—a marvellous and fearful fact!

If you and I can establish a sweet, attractive and finally glorious life, those around us will take note; as they follow in our steps they will be drawn in the same direction towards wisdom and lavish blessing, but in a greater measure than what we have ever attained.

Jesus placed a path beneath our feet.

His was a way of humility able to attract blessing into our lives. As He draws us into the right and narrow way, we may emulate His suffering for a little while, but the joy set before us is as it was for Him, a great motivator to endure. As we do, each successive generation will enjoy ever increasing levels of favour on earth and in heaven. What we are called to achieve is magnificent.

Who knew following would be so pivotal?

Who would have imagined a more beautiful piece of art as humility, suffering and glory are woven together in our lives, making us into the image of His dear son?

Is there any ceiling to this life and privilege we have been called up into?

Seemingly not, because there is far more of the Hero to take hold of.

We have followed His lead from His pre-incarnate life through the scripts. We have followed Him in His earthly example, now we must follow Him into the heavenlies.

John 14:12 | Hebrews 12:2 | Eph 3:18

As we press into Christ's inheritance before the Father, we experience the full height, depth and breadth of the love He bestows on His beloved son. As we dispossess Him by worshipfully inhabiting His place in the heavenlies and our life is hid with Christ in God, we leave a void in our lives on earth, ready for Christ the Son to rush into and fill.

In other words, Christ in us, the hope of glory.

The Hero Himself freely at work in and through us.

Who would have thought that a prostrate worshipper, caught up in the heavenlies within the Father's love, could create such potential within our own physical lives?

Now there is something for Christ to leverage in us, an opportunity for Him to express and realise His desires in our lives and our world—a way for Him to reach out and touch those close to us.

Through the Hero we move from glory to glory, we walk in authority, we find freedom and joy, and we enjoy a place of privilege both in the heavenlies and on earth.

Col 3:3 | Col 1:27 | Hebrews 13:21

Q1.   Who are the mothers and fathers in your life who have facilitated blessing in your life?

Q2.   Who stands on your shoulders?

Q3.   How will you contribute to inter-generational blessing within your family?

Prayer.

Lord. We want to sow our lives into generations to come. We pray for our children and their children. We intercede for our spiritual offspring and pray for humility, patience and tenacity as we labour spiritually so they can reap a plentiful inheritance of blessing. May it be, through Your hand on us, so that from this point on, all generations will call us blessed.   Amen.

HERO WORSHIP

And I thank Christ Jesus our Lord who has enabled me, because He counted me faithful, putting me into the ministry, although I was formerly a blasphemer, a persecutor, and an insolent man; but I obtained mercy because I did it ignorantly in unbelief. And the grace of our Lord was exceedingly abundant, with faith and love which are in Christ Jesus. This is a faithful saying and worthy of all acceptance, that Christ Jesus came into the world to save sinners, of whom I am chief. However, for this reason I obtained mercy, that in me first Jesus Christ might show all longsuffering, as a pattern to those who are going to believe on Him for everlasting life. Now to the King eternal, immortal, invisible, to God who alone is wise, be honor and glory forever and ever. Amen.

1 Timothy 1:12-17

Esther reveals Haman's Treason

The narrator sets the scene.

"Little did he know. One block away, a terrible enemy lurked . . ."

We, the audience are intrigued and gripped by the scene. We know so much, while the lead character bumbles blindly on, oblivious. We shout at the screen.

"Hurry up. When will you catch on?!"

"Watch out! They are right around the corner!"

We cringe. We groan when they make ridiculous decisions.

The scripts contextualise the circumstances of our lives. They punish every foolish act and reward every wise choice—propelling us forward along the path we have chosen.

The scripts narrate our stories. We watch each other, groan and shake our heads when others begin to fall from grace. The narration continues, as humankind struggles on oblivious. Creation looks on, wired to the heartbeat of those scripts. Creation groans too.

Little do we all know, but even if and when we grow in insight and try to do better, the groans continue. To know wisdom and the way of righteousness is one thing, to walk in it is something else entirely.

Then the Hero came onto the stage. He took the scripts that spoke of Him.

He fulfilled them.

Then He reworked them.

He achieved absolute mastery over them.

Now from the throne of heaven He uses them to draw us beyond the narrator's disapproval.

As we humbly heed His invitation we rise.

As He draws us up into the heavenlies, the narrators voice diminishes in the distance. Finally complete and glorious silence reigns.

Now another refrain rises to take its place—His words marking a different future for us . . .

"I give you authority, and I am with you always."

The basis for our newfound standing is His fulfilment of the scripts combined with our utter and complete dispossession of Christ in all things, as well as our unity with Him.

He is with us.

We are in Christ, seated with Him in heavenly places.

> We are part of His body, united with Him and in Him.

> We are in the beloved, and Christ is in us, the hope of glory.

The Hero came and took our future for Himself, He sacrificed His place and position to bring many sons and daughters to glory. He poured out the Holy Spirit on us so the architect of the scripts is again at the helm of our life. He passed on His authority so we can act for Him.

Finally He takes hold of us so we can share His life and so He shares ours.

We are placed squarely into the hero script, so we can walk comfortably forward into favour and blessing. It is generous, more than generous. It is utterly remarkable!

One final idea captures my imagination more than anything. It is the subject of this book's final section. It brings me to a deep place of worship, beyond reason, a place where I am drawn into thankfulness and a joyous response to unconditional love as I realise that our lives are entangled with the life of the Hero Himself—a breath-taking, beautiful and inconceivable potential.

PART
5

THE HERO WITHIN

HERO WORSHIP

And being in Bethany at the house of Simon the leper, as He sat at the table, a woman came having an alabaster flask of very costly oil of spikenard. Then she broke the flask and poured it on His head. But there were some who were indignant among themselves, and said, "Why was this fragrant oil wasted? For it might have been sold for more than three hundred denarii and given to the poor." And they criticized her sharply.

But Jesus said, "Let her alone. Why do you trouble her? She has done a good work for Me. For you have the poor with you always, and whenever you wish you may do them good; but Me you do not have always. She has done what she could. She has come beforehand to anoint My body for burial. Assuredly, I say to you, wherever this gospel is preached in the whole world, what this woman has done will also be told as a memorial to her."

Mark 14:3-9

Christ in the Synagogue

CHAPTER FORTY-FIVE

THE FATHER INCARNATE

HE VOLUNTARILY CONTINUED TO SPEAK AND
ACT IN ACCORDANCE WITH THE FATHER'S
WORDS AND ACTIONS EXPRESSED IN HIS BODY.

Everyone went to their own home, but Jesus went to the Mount of Olives—His sacred space. As He draws near to His father, the physical demands of the day diminish. I imagine Him entering into the heavenlies, and perhaps for the entire night He watches His father at work. They speak together, and His father's words linger in His soul.

All of this is fresh in His mind when He comes back into the town at dawn, only to walk straight into the trap some religious leaders had carefully laid for Him—a set-up in the form of a public stoning of an adulterous woman. As we know, Jesus engaged with the situation with a wisdom that was entirely heavenly—He defused the threat to the woman and, against all odds, walked away with His reputation intact as well.

Christ spent the rest of that day with one purpose. He wanted everyone to know that His words and actions were not His own—they had come from His father. It seems His experience in the heavenlies the previous night had primed Him so that He knew the exact words and actions that were needed to successfully navigate whatever came next.

Having entered the Father's house while everyone else was asleep, He came out with razor-sharp clarity, fully resourced for the day ahead. What an incredible and admirable lifestyle!

John 7:53-8:30

Awesome, right? And what a wonderful ideal for us to pursue—to be often found entering the courts above, comfortable in the Father's heavenly mountain home.

Yet, we need to go deeper and further to keep up with Him . . .

When Christ went to prayer, His spirit entered right in to the Father's presence. And as He pushed in to the heavenlies to take hold of the life of His father, some little part of His earthly life was displaced—a void that could be filled by the Father's spirit. Now Christ carried the potential for the Father to express Himself in His life the following day. Desire for the Father drew him. His father knew what the next day promised for His son, so He welcomed Him home and set Him up for victory even while others were plotting His downfall. The Father knew what was coming—and determined that He would personally intervene.

And He did! The darkness faded with the dawn and Jesus soon found Himself among the crowd. He walked into the trap they had laid for Him—choose between God and the Roman oppressor. In the tension of the moment, what He said and did came as a surprise and a delight, even to Him! It impressed Him so much, He literally raved the rest of the day about what had happened. His father had taken over, a reality entirely delightful to a devoted Son! He wanted everyone to understand.

He had experienced a strange and lovely compulsion . . . a compulsion born out of unity, and intertwined lives.

We need to linger here because this is something we need to grapple with in our own lives, but I believe the best place to begin is to reflect on how this dynamic fits amongst the other elements at play in the life and ministry of Jesus.

Here they are:

1. **Identity**—Jesus was living out a continuation of His story. He was the Hero from before the beginning, Jehovah, the Old Testament 'Angel of the Lord.'

2. **Form**—He had laid aside divinity and taken flesh. He had a human body.

Isa 2:3 | Zech 8:3 | John 8:58 | Gen 16, 22 & 32 | Exod 3 | Josh 5:13-15 |1 Sam 17:45
John 1:1-14 | Phil 2:5-11

3. **The Holy Spirit**—He was indwelt with the Spirit of God for life and ministry in the same way as many of the greats of the Old Testament were.

4. **Authority**—His identity lent Him authority over sickness and the darkness. They knew who He was.

5. **Angels**—Angels served Him, protected Him, and at times participated in the miracles He performed.

6. **The Scripts**—He played the part of the Hero (and also the part of the villain), and as He did so, the power of the scripts was manifest, in terms of favour and blessing.

7. **The Father**—Through unity and connection with His father in heaven, His words and actions were augmented at times, to release wisdom and power on a whole other level.

Granted, this is a more complex way to view Christ's ministry—much more complicated than the understanding I was brought up with. For us back then, it was simple. Jesus just did amazing stuff because He was God and God has awesome power. We still appreciate those perspectives, however there are more nuances to His life to delight our hearts if we only dig deeper.

As we search, we find truth to inform our destiny as sons and daughters of the living God and we are empowered to accept the call to be conformed to the image of His dear son. We need more than a simple story, or we will find it impossible to get the job done. In fact, deficient thinking on our part might well stymie the Lord's ability to accomplish His purpose in us.

Christ's connection to the Father surfaced through what I have come to refer to as 'compulsive behaviour.' Whenever He felt His father reaching for control, He submitted, leaning into that wonderful compulsion. Jesus allowed His father to take over and direct His words and actions—He voluntarily continued to speak and act in accordance with His father's will as it was expressed in His body. Adding in this perspective, we might summarise it this way:

"I hear My father speak [through My mouth], and I speak. I see what My father does [through My body] and I act in accordance."

Luke 4:14, 18-19 | Matt 8 | John 5, 8 & 14

Even though . . .

> *No one has seen God at any time. The only begotten Son, who is in the*
> *bosom of the Father, He has declared Him.   John 1:18*

And . . .

> *. . . for no man shall see Me, and live."   Exodus 33:20*

And . . .

> *[He] alone has immortality, dwelling in unapproachable light, whom*
> *no man has seen or can see . . .   1 Timothy 6:16*

Even though the Father is hidden and unapproachable, through the dynamics of a united life, Jesus became His mouthpiece and His hands and feet in the world. The one who was eternally beyond knowledge spoke words with a human mouth, and touched humanity with human fingertips!

Q1.   Is Christ your example? What does this day in His life mean to you as you think of the day ahead?

Q2.   Consider the list of elements in play in the life and ministry of Jesus. Which of them have you experienced yourself?

Q3.   What do you know of the compulsion described in this chapter? Have you ever felt it and how did you respond? What happened next?

Prayer.

Lord. There are people around us in need of Your touch. There are those who are desperate to hear You speak over them. We open ourselves up to you. We submit to what You want to do in and through our mouths and bodies. Help us find our place in the sacred space, so we can leave room for You in all of our life and walk and calling. Bind us to heaven, and draw us into the secret place. Intertwine our lives with Your own. Help us to live in the presence and grant us rich experience of the draw and power of Your love.   Amen.

CHAPTER FORTY-SIX

THE COMPULSION OF CHRIST

READING THE EXPECTATION IN HER VOICE AND
REALISING HER THOUGHTS HAVE FOUND THEIR
WAY TO THE MIRACULOUS, HE HESITATES.

To take these ideas further, let's explore a few key moments in the ministry of Jesus. As we read the stories about Him, it surprises us to discover they make more sense as we slide a lens of the *compulsion of Christ* over them.

For example . . .

Jesus had just begun His ministry. It felt uncomfortable—this was a huge life change for Him. He was yet to grow accustomed or feel at ease with the significant decisions He had recently made. He had stepped from under the shadow of His cousin, John the Baptist. He had taken on the role of Rabbi. He had called His disciples, and as we locate Him in scripture, we find Him distracted by questions of what was to come. He was in a preparation phase. In His mind, His time was not yet come. He had uncomfortably stepped out into the no man's land of His *now-but-not-yet*. This was important and He knew it, hence His single-minded focus.

Suddenly, and not really by choice, He is caught up by the bustle of a family wedding in Cana.

Next, they run out of wine. He hardly heard His mother's words quietly in His ear.

He had never had to worry about logistics quite like this. He remembered how He had stepped up when His adopted father had passed away. It had been such hard work to fill the void Joseph had left, to care for His mother and

John 2:1-11

siblings in place of a man who had been such a rock in their life. Sure, there had been grief, and the sheer responsibilities had pressed down, overly heavy throughout a painful season, but these days seemed strangely even more difficult—a completely different trajectory and a lack of sense of next steps. Trust. He would trust His father, as was His habit.

Mary is urgent and impatient. She leans in close to quietly interrupt. A glimmer of shame in her tone helps to get His attention. Quietly forceful, even insistent, she suggests He lend a hand. Still distracted at the challenge of a dozen of His own mouths to feed in future days, He brushes off her request. Not long ago He had fasted forty days in the wilderness. Wine and a feast—they were not really His priority. Reading the expectation in her voice and realising her thoughts had found their way to the miraculous, He hesitates. No. He has heard from His father, whose last words were for Him to wait until His time was come.

Jesus' answer to His mother was therefore "No!" . . . but then His body and mouth act of their own accord. He stands and walks across the room, gives instructions to the servants and performs His first miracle.

It seems Mum and Dad had formed an alliance, teaming up to give the young messiah a push towards His destiny . . .

Christ's first miracle was not in His plan. He found Himself doing and saying unexpected and unintended things—and soon the wine was flowing again.

As I write this, I linger in the wonder of the moment, yet there is more, so we must press on.

Another example in Christ's life, some years later is just as simple and clear.

We find Jesus in conversation with His disciples. They ask and He answers . . .

"No, I will not come to the feast."

After their objections are heard, and when He insists, they go on without Him.

Then He goes up to feast anyway.

"Hang on a second. What just happened?"

I know, right? Christ either lied or changed His mind.

John 2:1-11 | John 7:8-10

The first is impossible and the second is unexpected behaviour for the Son of God. We would expect Him to be more organised in His mind.

Outside our compulsion paradigm we would be at a loss to explain this, but suddenly we feel chuffed, because our point of view allows Christ to remain both sinless and exemplary.

Christ had a plan. He would stay away. He was only too aware of the extent of their plots to kill Him. He also knew this wasn't His time to die. His choice not to go was an act of obedience and humility.

The next thing He knew, He was on His feet in the middle of the Temple at the busiest time of the feast. He wasn't even on the periphery, discrete and unobtrusive. This was exactly the opposite of what He had chosen!

Suddenly He addresses the crowd. Apprehension gives way to joy as He feels His father flow through Him. He begins to teach and it is a whole other level, even for Him!

His words blow His audience away.

"What's with His knowledge of scripture and theology . . . and with no formal education?" they ask.

Jesus responds.

"This is not My teaching," He says. "My teaching is not My own, but His who sent me."

He goes on to confirm that His words were not of His own accord, nor by His own authority.

Instead, someone else had momentarily taken the lead—the direction of the life and ministry of the messiah, the Son of God was in the hands of another. The Father had something to say, and He took over. He propelled Christ to travel to a place at a time in contradiction to His plans. He spoke His own words and brought wisdom that was entirely heavenly in origin to earth. No one could believe what they heard. Christ Himself refused to take credit. The interplay between Father and Son is absolutely captivating. This is not the only dynamic behind the wonderful words and miracles of Christ, but it is the one most able to capture my imagination.

John 7:6-9 | John 7:15-16

And the Father does not stop with Jesus. Peter also takes his turn to enjoy a heavenly takeover.

"Who do you say that I am?" Jesus asks.

Peter is interested in the question, but unsure of how to respond, just like the rest of the disciples. It is his habit to speak before he thinks, but this was more extreme by far . . .

"You are the Christ, the Son of the living God!"

"Whoa! What did I just say?" Peter thinks.

Jesus affirms him, speaking from His own experience, only too aware of the dynamic at work.

"Blessed are you, Simon son of Jonah, for this was not revealed to you by flesh and blood, but by My father in heaven."

"Revealed?" Peter thinks. "It just came out without even entering my head."

When the Father wanted to say something about Jesus, He just took over Peter's mouth for a moment.

My last example from the life of Christ is my favourite. In Luke chapter ten, the seventy return to Jesus full of joy. They are ecstatic as they proclaim, "Lord, even the demons are subject to us in Your name."

Then Jesus speaks:

> "I saw Satan fall like lightning from heaven. Behold, I give you the
> authority to trample on serpents and scorpions, and over all the power
> of the enemy, and nothing shall by any means hurt you. Nevertheless do
> not rejoice in this, that the spirits are subject to you, but rather rejoice
> because your names are written in heaven."

This sounds like an encouragement mixed with gentle direction, the act of a mentor who cares, but there was more in play.

To see it, look at Christ's response to His own words. He prays, in an ecstasy before the Father, hardly aware of His audience.

Matt 16:13-20 | Luke 10:17-24

"What just happened?"

Let's listen in to His prayer.

> In that hour Jesus rejoiced in the Spirit and said, "I thank You,
> Father, Lord of heaven and earth, that You have hidden these
> things from the wise and prudent and revealed them to babes.
> Even so, Father, for so it seemed good in Your sight. All things
> have been delivered to Me by My Father, and no one knows who
> the Son is except the Father, and who the Father is except the
> Son, and the one to whom the Son wills to reveal Him."

The Father used His son's mouth to declare and release protection and authority into the disciple's lives. Christ found Himself taken over by the One who desired to release a tremendous blessing over them. When He realised His words were not His own, He was suddenly caught up in agreement with what had just happened. Breaking into worship, His heart is overcome and He rejoices greatly as He considers what His declaration would mean for the disciples' future.

"Yes, it really is true! I have been given the authority to declare those words over My beloved disciples. Wow! What an awesome thing to say, Father. It's perfect! I couldn't have said it better myself. So good!"

I imagine the disciples as they looked on in awe. What kind of delicious madness was before them, as they watched their deeply revered teacher apparently talking to Himself?

Luke 10:21-22

Q1.   How are you practically connected to heaven??

Q2.   Do you think there have been times when your desire to obey has hindered what the Father wants to do through you?

Q3.   Reflect on the outcomes of the Father's words and actions in Christ's life as described here, and their relationship with worship and wonder?

Prayer.

Lord. We want to live beyond ourselves. We submit to a greater wisdom and a heart richer in passion and power. We want You to take over our duties and do better. We want You to change us from being a spectator—to take a pivotal and active role in the fulfilment of Your desire to release joy and cheer in this world. Grace us so our hesitation gives way to the one who has no relationship with fear. Father, overwhelm us with Your passion to do good in this world.   Amen.

CHAPTER FORTY-SEVEN

INTERTWINED LIVES

IT IS NOT COMFORTABLE TO BE OVERTAKEN
BY ANOTHER—TO LOSE CONTROL OF OUR
LIFE TO THE ONE WHO WE HAVE WELCOMED
IN.

For each of the churches in the book of Revelation, Jesus offers a token to the one who overcomes. This is what He says to the church in Laodicea:

> *Behold, I stand at the door and knock. If anyone hears My voice and*
> *opens the door, I will come in to him and dine with him, and he with*
> *Me. To him who overcomes I will grant to sit with Me on My throne,*
> *as I also overcame and sat down with My Father on His throne.*

The mechanism of Christ's shared life with the Father is the same as the one which operates between Him and us now.

Jesus tells us that He is in the Father and the Father is in Him. Their relationship was a mutual blessing, and it brought heaven to earth but the dynamics that made it so wonderful were complex—their lives were intertwined across the divide between the physical and the unseen.

We are in Christ. The New Testament is peppered with the phrase. It is equally true that He is in us. It's not just the Holy Spirit, but Christ who lives in us. Christ in you, the hope of glory. Again, intertwined lives!

The mechanism behind Christ's compulsion as the Father acted and spoke through Him was their interconnected lives—a unity somehow centred in a shared throne. The Father sat on the throne in heaven and Christ shared His place because He was *in the Father.*

Rev 3:20-21 | John 14:11 | 2 Cor 5:17 | Rom 8:1 | John 15:5 | Gal 3:26

It worked for Him just as it does for us. We are in the beloved. We are in Christ. We are pictured in Christ, seated with Him in heavenly places.

Christ and His father in Heaven. Us and our unity with Christ in His exalted state. The pairing dynamics are the same—one is seated on the throne in Heaven with their life there, the other is on the earth with their life here. The two are connected and the throne is shared. The throne-sitter is in the earth-walker and vice versa.

The Laodicean church was troubled with hesitation in their spiritual walk. Jesus invited them to be all-in in their faith. If they would forsake their lukewarm attitudes and become wholehearted they could enjoy the wonder of His shared throne and a life intertwined with His own.

"Share My throne, just as I shared My father's throne. I have this as a prize for the overcomer who leaves behind an insipid and weak faith-walk—a reward for those who embrace the uncomfortable extremes you have begun to experience."

Christ tries to get through in the lives of the Laodicean Christians, but the compulsion associated with that is more than awkward. They find words on their lips that they never meant to say. They have new and weird impulses. So far they have managed to keep the apparent madness of the compulsion at bay but it's caused them to shrink back.

They fight to settle themselves down. They battle to control themselves—to stick to the known quality of a lukewarm status quo, they shun the extremes, until Jesus speaks . . .

"I stand at the door, and knock. I want to come into your life."

"And I want to invite you up into Mine."

"Share My throne and My place in the heavenlies, but do so at the cost of your life! I want in!"

"I want in, and to embrace My life is to give yours away . . . to submit to the compulsion of My will as I live in and through your life.

We too hear His voice, a humble request for entrance. Destinies await when we heed the call and swing the door wide—a moment, a meeting of humble hearts.

Eph 1:3, 6 & 2:6 | Rev 3:14-22

We hear His voice, here in the book of Revelation, "Behold I stand at the door and knock."

In other places the voice of Christ speaks similarly but with other language. "Enter in," He says in John chapter eleven, as He invites us to find pasture and enjoy His abundant life for us. In the book of Hebrews, to enter in is to cross the Jordan and find a place in the Promised Land. If we hear and heed His voice, we come into the heavenlies, to Mt Zion, to the presence of the Lord and His angels, and the vast assembly of the righteous.

The voice of Christ is one message with twin refrains—"Let Me in," and "Enter in."

They are one and the same because the two actions are linked. This is about our assent to practical unity with the risen and glorious enthroned Lord Jesus— intertwined lives.

Christ in you and me, and our place in Him, in His body.

It's not automatic. It requires a nod of our head.

This is our inheritance; the fulfilment of every promise is hidden behind this door. Here there is abundance, pasture, and the end of want, lack and thirst. This is the pearl of great price, the treasure hid in the field, and life in all its fulness.

A simple *yes*, elevates us to being seated with Christ in heavenly places where we are welcome to explore the height, depth, length and breadth of the Father's great love lavished on His beloved son—every spiritual blessing in heavenly places. This is an entrance to live at an entirely new level.

But here's the rub. It is not easy, nor comfortable to be overtaken by another— to lose control of our life to the one who we have welcomed in.

It is fire and ice rather than the comfortable tepid temperature of the safe life we would choose if left to ourselves.

The book of Hebrews warns us. If we hear His voice we should not harden our hearts. Others failed to enter. The Hebrew believers too would find no rest if they chose to resist the new and uncomfortable compulsions Christ was releasing into their lives.

Rev 3:20 | John 10:1-10 | Matt 13:44-46 | Eph 2:6 | Eph 3:18 | Rev 3:15-16 | Heb 3

We don't like the way it feels. We naturally and almost involuntarily resist Christ when he reaches for the controls of our life. The compulsion and the seemingly unpleasant extremes, we find no pleasure in them. And He doesn't like the way it feels either when we resist. "I find no pleasure in those who shrink back," He remarks.

To reject the invitation, and hold out on Christ is to be distasteful to Him, hence His words, "I will spew you out of My mouth!"

This is not easy, but there is no more significant moment than when we find ourselves out of our depth. With a niggle, we feel our control slip away, confronted by an deep impulse to say and do things very much beyond our plans and purposes, and distinctly out of our comfort zone.

Heb 10:38 | Rev 3:16

Q1.   What does "seated with Christ in heavenly places" mean to you?

Q2.   Which do you find more of a draw to your heart, our live in Christ in the heavenlies or His life in ours on earth?

Q3.   How do you keep your life between the lines? What do you need to lay down in order to pick up the key and unlock the door of your heart and life?

Prayer.

Lord. Come in. You are invited into our lives in every aspect and without reserve. We welcome Your rule and reign, Lord Jesus — in our lives and in our futures, and in our families, and in our world. Come, Lord Jesus!   Amen.

CHAPTER FORTY-EIGHT

EQUAL AND OPPOSITE

THE PROPORTION OF HIS LIFE I TAKE
FROM HIM IS EQUIVALENT TO THE VOID
I LEAVE FOR HIM IN MY OWN.

In chemistry class early on in high school, it seemed to be anyone's guess what would happen when you mixed two chemicals together. The equations did my head in and felt quite random. Still, the teacher taught and we eventually we learned many of the patterns and rules that govern chemical reactions. We began to get the hang of how it all worked . . .

We learned that matter is in fact neither created nor destroyed within chemical reactions. The atoms themselves, the elements, are not transformed into other elements—instead they are preserved and bound together in predictable combinations. So whether we explode the science lab, bake a cake, or manufacture a type of plastic, what goes into the mix is transformed but also preserved.

In another class, physics this time, there were other rules to take on board, like: "For every action there is an equal and opposite reaction."

What's the point? Only this: in the physical world incredibly powerful and transformative things can occur, and amongst the apparent randomness and complexity of what happens, balance and order exist.

The same is true of the dynamics that govern our relationship with Christ.

His life and ours come together. It's a powerful interaction. Its transformative. There is a balance and an order to our dance with the divine, a rhythm and predictability.

Both are changed. Both are preserved.

It is equal and opposite . . .

The embrace of intertwined lives is proportional.

When I actively engage with my life in Christ. When I step into the heavenlies. When I choose to withdraw from this world, from my physical life, and take my place in the life of Christ . . .

. . . I dispossess Him from His life above;

. . . I create a void in my life below;

. . . The proportion of His life I take from Him is equivalent to the void I leave for Him in my own down here.

I step higher and take His place and position and He stoops to take mine. I receive His abundant life, His honour, His authority and enjoy refreshment in my spirit and the affirmation of the Father's love as I inhabit His place and position. He takes my want, my weakness, my failure, my regrettable consequences, my cares and my need.

Christ and we are not equal in and of ourselves. What passes between us, however, *is* equal. —even when a planet and a pebble collide, the forces they exert on each other are equal and opposite.

When the Lord revealed this to me, I played around with it. I thought this mutual displacement might be equal and opposite in terms of time. At first I figured if I took five minutes to step into His life . . . Jesus would take over my life simultaneously, while I was sort of absent, busy in the spirit.

I was wrong.

I tried it and nothing seemed to happen.

I continued to press in, beyond my reason and understanding . . . in pursuit of how it all might work. Little did I know. I had built up a significant potential in my life and He could choose to inhabit it at will.

I kept on. I'd steal brief moments —as much as I could.

Invisibly and indiscernibly, a deficit in my life began to cry out to be rebalanced.

When it resolved it came like a heavenly avalanche—a great wave of compulsion!

This is what happened.

We had been in prayer for a troubled young woman who we had met over coffee earlier in the day. Anya and I were given some discernment for her, a little of the prophetic and a real touch of the presence of the Holy Spirit. He was obviously ready to move in her life. We were used to His ways. Good. Fine. It wasn't too much trouble to drink good coffee and pray for someone, right?

Then we went to an event with this woman and she sat with us. Afterwards, as we parted, Anya offered for us to pray for her once more.

I nodded to myself. One more prayer was a great idea, and she accepted our offer.

We invited a wonderful, spirit-filled friend to join us in the busy corridor. Anya prayed first, and I prayed alongside silently, but I have to admit, I wasn't exactly fully engaged in the moment.

My turn.

I can't remember what I prayed but I remember I felt slightly distracted and feeble. The last word of my own was a simple command, "Out!"

Suddenly I got hit. In hindsight, it was the potential I had built up for the last few weeks.

Christ choose the moment to take over . . .

A flood of other-worldly language came out of my mouth.

I was nearly knocked over. The woman began to sink down. She came to rest with her face down on her knees. Our friend, conscious of the people all around us helped get us all into a private room. The truth was, I was not in control of my faculties. Someone else was. I needed help to move, even to be aware of the need of privacy.

Another torrent of heavenly commands, and then she began to cough violently. Again she sank down to the floor, only this time, she was at peace.

Christ had come. The Hero was busy ministering into her life.

Suddenly it was over, the woman was up on her feet and we said goodbye once more.

A few minutes later, our world was apparently back to normal, but I wasn't. I was staggered inside. To be frank, I was a little embarrassed. The last ten minutes had been amazing but I had been doing things and saying things . . . that weren't my choice. I had allowed Christ entrance, but my choices from that point on had become entirely irrelevant.

I walked away from the experience worried about what I might do next, or more precisely, what Christ might do next when He took over again, which could be anytime . . . when I least expected it.

Scarily unpredictable—Yes.

Random—No!

Days later, a realisation dawned on my rattled brain. It wasn't random. I had taken hold of Christ's life time after time in my silly little experiments, and He had taken my life-deficit back, all at once!

Paul puts it this way,

> *For he who sows to his flesh will of the flesh reap corruption, but he*
> *who sows to the Spirit will of the Spirit reap everlasting life. And let*
> *us not grow weary while doing good, for in due season we shall reap if*
> *we do not lose heart.*

It overpowered me, but there was a proportionality to it. It was equal and opposite.

He started it, and in the end, He chose the time and place, and even the intensity. Yet somewhere in the middle I had a choice, a chance to respond and requite His desire for me with my desire for Him.

He knocked and I opened the door.

It was a two-way street. As we move forward, the extent of our continued passion to sow into this becomes a question for us all. Will we build a dispossession potential—a powerful enticement for Christ to come again and again, until His rule and reign becomes a lifestyle?

Gal 6:8-9 | Rev 3:20

Q1.   What is the greatest testimony you carry of the Lord at work in and around you?

Q2.   How do you sow in the spirit in this season of your life?

Q3.   When were you last shocked by what the Lord did through you? What happened?

Prayer.

Lord. Thank You that You never say to us, "This far and no further." We push in to know more of You and Your ways. We want to lay hold of those things that You had in mind when You laid hold of us. We want to live out our potential but we are beginning to understand that our potential is not limited by what is in us. Our ceiling is limitless because we are bound to the King of heaven. We step back so that You can live out Your potential though us.   Amen.

CHAPTER FORTY-NINE

AN ORDER OF MAGNITUDE

**EVEN THOUGH THE WAY HE DRIVES
US SEEMS A LITTLE RECKLESS, WE
CRY OUT, "COME LORD JESUS!"**

The risen and glorified Lord Jesus, and the hero of every story from before time began until the future culmination of all things, has positioned us as an outpost from which He works out His desire for the people of this world.

For Him to get His way, we need to concede our lives, but we are more than recompensed. We win in both directions—when we take hold of the life of Christ in the heavenlies and also when He takes hold of ours on earth.

When we lose our lives we save them, because the life we press into is of another order of magnitude to the one we relinquish, and the one who takes residence in our lives is of another order of magnitude in terms of His spirit and person.

In ages past He was the Hero, and then the Creator whose fingers worked this world into being. Then He was Jehovah with the capacity as a divine being to take hold of a nation and shape their destiny even while He held enemy superpowers and their gods at bay.

Later He was the incarnate Son of God who became our Saviour. He cast out demons, expounded the kingdom, multiplied food, walked on water, healed the sick, raised the dead and completely decimated the defences of the darkness.

Then He was the one who rose again, walked through walls or clean disappeared and then rose into heaven at will.

Now He has been given all authority and reigns over all things.

Matt 16:25 | Ps 8:3 | Exod 7-11 | Matt 5, 8 | John 20-Acts 1:11 | 1 Cor 15:25-28

The potential of what could happen if He took hold of our lives for even a few moments is beyond understanding.

From that point on, nothing can be impossible.

There are . . .

No questions around what should and could happen.

No authority deficit.

No end of power or legitimacy.

There is no problem in my life or the lives of those around me able to cause Him to miss a beat. He who appears as molten from the waist down, the one who presides amongst the candle sticks, is limitless, wise beyond measure, and always the hero.

He who is the 'desire of nations' comes to take hold of you and me, and though the way He drives sometimes seems a little reckless with little regard for our boundaries or reputation, still we cry out, "Come Lord Jesus!"

Or even, "Jesus take the wheel!"

Peter was in jail. His friend and fellow leader of the early church had just been killed. Peter knew he was the second act of Herod's vendetta against the church, but he slept well until Jesus took the opportunity to take over. Peter's experience was a sort of trancelike out of body experience. He was in the spirit. An angel guided him through broken bonds and open gates. Taking over his physical body, Jesus easily navigated Peter out of the prison. Somewhere down the road, Peter comes out of his trance and Jesus and he swap back their places now that his situation is resolved. Someone of another magnitude entirely took over and effortlessly resolved his life-threatening circumstances.

It works in our favour in the other direction too. No matter how small and constrained our lives are on earth, as we press in, we find ourselves in an expansive world of blessing, a world the Father has bequeathed to His beloved son. We share the throne, for goodness sake!—every spiritual blessing in heavenly places, in the Beloved. We are rooted and grounded in love—the atmosphere of the Father's house—and that love permeates the very fabric of the place in every respect.

Rev 1:12-16 | Acts 12 | Eph 2:6 | Eph 1:3-6 | Eph 3:17

Robed in righteousness we feast at His table—there is no want or lack, just abundance and satisfaction. This is our home, a life hidden with Christ in God.

As we give up our lives to take hold of Christ's, this heavenly principle guides our expectations:

> *Give, and it will be given to you: good measure, pressed*
> *down, shaken together, and running over will be put*
> *into your bosom. For with the same measure that you*
> *use, it will be measured back to you."*

Somewhere here is a delightful paradox able to broadside us all—humility is the key to everything. Humility guided the Hero early, and humility encourages us now to follow His lead and give away our lives to make room for Him. Yet in the end as we reap the fruit of humility we are overwhelmed because blessing follows hard on its heels.

Peter once reflected on the cost of discipleship at Christ's side:

> *Then Peter began to say to Him, "See, we have left all and followed*
> *You." So Jesus answered and said, "Assuredly, I say to you, there*
> *is no one who has left house or brothers or sisters or father or*
> *mother or wife or children or lands, for My sake and the gospel's,*
> *who shall not receive a hundredfold now in this time—houses and*
> *brothers and sisters and mothers and children and lands, with*
> *persecutions—and in the age to come, eternal life. But many who*
> *are first will be last, and the last first."*

Notice the hundred-fold recompense. We have talked about Christ and His life being of another order of magnitude to us and our life. In ordinary understanding, another order of magnitude is a ten-fold multiplication. Christ's response to Peter shows us the spiritual principle—a guide for our expectations in terms of compensation. It is two orders of magnitude greater than what we sacrifice—as we place our lives on the altar and welcome Christ's rule and reign. The return is a hundred-fold both in this life (His person expressed in my life) and the life to come (my experience of His life as I walk in the spirit and clothe myself with Christ).

Luke 15:22-24 | Psa 23 | 2 Sam 9:13 | Luke 6:38 | Gal 6:8b-9 | Mark 10:28-31

I find myself with the question, "How much of my time, my being, my energy, my strength, soul and spirit can I stuff into His life in the unseen realm?"

When I enter in, I win.

When He takes my place, I win.

And when I lose my life and find it elsewhere . . . I also win.

Our impact for the kingdom is magnified at least one hundred fold above what we might accomplish outside of Christ, and our enrichment in terms of joy and privilege as we live out of His place in the joy of God is greater still as we lean in to take hold of His life.

Q1.   Do you see the life of Christ in heaven to be greater, richer and more expansive than your own? Why, or why not?

Q2.   Is an experience of the life of Christ through His body in the heavenlies accessible for you? What is your experience of these things? How would you lead others in this?

Q3.   What choices can you make to stuff more of yourself into the unseen, so as to leave more room for Christ to inhabit your life? What are your expectations of Him as He responds in kind?

Prayer.

Lord. Our hearts are restless till they find their rest in You. Your life is the sabbath we seek, for we crave what the world cannot satisfy. Welcome us into Your joy, into the rest You have for the people of God. And take Your place in us. May we be fit temples for Your habitation. Sanctify us according to Your truth. Bring us to life and immortality. Overflow the feeble capacity of our frail and finite flesh. Let the glorious light of Your presence shine out of us as You speak and act through us. We offer these bodies as living sacrifices. Conform us to Your image, we pray.   Amen.

CHAPTER FIFTY

CRACKED POTS

PAUL WAS RUSHING HEADLONG AND POURING
HIMSELF OUT WITH THE SAME END IN MIND,
BUT SO MUCH MORE PASSION FOR IT!.

Paul missed the training course. "I am an apostle born out of due time," he declared. The others had walked with Jesus but he had to make do with a brilliant and blinding encounter with the risen and glorified Christ on the road to Damascus.

He was little aware of how extraordinarily successful in his role he was. He left a legacy to this world surpassed only by Christ Himself. Even so, the longer he pursued his call, the more constrained his life became. Persecution and torture and long periods of imprisonment became his new normal.

Somehow, the more difficult it all became, the stronger his light shone.

Paul constantly referred to a new reality—an experience of a life lived "in Christ"—and in his letters he explores what it means to live out of relationship, "in the beloved and in the heavenlies."

Perhaps his most profound words are these:

> That I may know Him and the power of His resurrection, and the
> fellowship of His sufferings, being conformed to His death.

To lose our lives to find them is a matter of degrees. While I was on the watch for potential moments to push into Christ's life above, as an experiment to welcome the person of Jesus into my life, Paul was rushing headlong and

1 Cor 15:8 | Acts 9 | Eph 1:3-6, 2:6 | Phil 3:10

pouring himself out as a drink offering. He had the same end in mind, but so much more passion for it!

And so we step in. We lose ourselves in worship. We walk the streets of Zion in order to know and experience what it means to be in Christ. We forsake houses and farms, loved ones and family. We suffer scorn and ridicule. We suffer brutal persecution and injury. We give our lives, we give our all.

It's a matter of degrees, a continuum of cause and effect. Paul was at the far end of the sliding-scale as he tried for all he was worth to take hold of Jesus. He found Him as he was beaten, as they stoned him, and in the long years of forced imprisonment.

As he suffered, he pursued identification with the incarnate Jesus, whom he never met physically. There he also met Him in His resurrection and felt Him take over and live through him—his persecutors would leave him for dead but in and through Christ, he would just get up and walk away.

In Second Corinthians he talks about earthen pots. The more we are broken, he explains, the more the life of Jesus shines through.

Paul lived for the moments when Christ would take hold of him. He said, "I want to take hold of that which is the reason for which Christ took hold of me," or in the words of Francis Ridley Havergal's hymn,

> *"Jesus, take my will and make it Thine, it shall be no longer mine. Take my heart it is thine own; it shall be thy royal throne. Take my love, my Lord I pour at your feet its treasure store. Take myself and I will be ever, only all for thee . . ."*

John the Baptist said it like this: "He must increase, and I must decrease."

Paul's broken pots was an allusion to the story of Gideon who won a battle, but not through weapons or military skill or strategy.

No, he look some lamps and put them in pots. He and a few companions snuck up on the enemy camp . . .

They shattered those pots, suddenly revealing . . .

the hidden light inside.

2 Tim 4:6 | Acts 14:19-23 2 Cor 4:6-18 | Phil 3:12 | John 3:30 | Judges 7

His illuminating surprise and the sound of the trumpets they blew completely turned the tide of the war.

Suddenly light shattered the darkness.

The enemy fled.

The light hidden within the clay pots was released; the outcome of the war was no longer a question of military prowess and strategy as that inner light overcame the darkness.

Gideon was called a mighty warrior by the Lord—a prophesy fulfilled by him as he brought the light and not the fight to the enemy.

The same is true for us.

We spend a lot of time focussed on the will of God—we hear and obey His voice. For Paul, the will of God was fulfilled in his life at the times when Christ shone through, until he was hidden in shadow.

Perhaps we need not go to the same lengths as this super-saint, but I feel inclined to believe we would all do well to live life in roughly the same direction.

Judges 7:22

Q1.   In what way do you feel like you are a cracked earthen vessel?

Q2.   How have you invested in your ability to carry the light?

Q3.   What tension exists in you between what God has spoken over you and who you appear to be? Explain how can this be resolved by the reality of Christ in you.

Prayer.

Lord. You are the servant-king and we bring our cracked and broken vessels to You to be filled. Thank you. You inhabit earth and clay. You are the breath and the light and the life—enough to make a vessel unto honour from something once lowly and base. Thank you. Your strength is made perfect in the weakness of who we are. We take heart for we know the truth—we the people who know our God shall be strong and do great exploits, as You live in and through us.   Amen.

CHAPTER FIFTY-ONE

LOST IN HIM

EVERY GOOD THING CAN BE TRACED
BACK SOMEHOW TO ONE OF HIS
HEROIC DECISIONS OR ACTS.

In a previous chapter, we considered the factors at play in the life and ministry of Jesus.

Here they are again:

1. **Identity** — Jesus lived out a continuation of His own story. He was the Hero from before the beginning, Jehovah and the Angel of the Lord of the Old Testament.

2. **Form** — He had laid aside divinity and taken flesh — a human body.

3. **The Holy Spirit** — We was indwelt with the Spirit of God for life and ministry in the same way as many of the greats of the Old Testament were.

4. **Authority** — His identity lent Him authority over sickness and the darkness. They knew who He was.

5. **Angels** — Angels served Him and protected Him and at times participated in the miracles He performed.

6. **The Scripts** — He played the part of the Hero (and also the part of the villain), and as He did so the power of the scripts was manifest, in terms of favour and blessing.

Gen 16, 22 & 32 | Exod 3 | Josh 5:13-15 |1 Sam 17:45 John 1:1-14 | Phil 2:5-11
Luke 4:14, 18-19 | Matt 8

7. **The Father**—Through unity and connection with His father in heaven, His words and actions were augmented at times by Him, to release wisdom and power on a whole other level.

In light of all we have discussed, it is helpful, I believe, to reflect on these elements available for us as well in our lives:

1. **Identity**—Through dispossession of Christ and unity in Him we are sons and daughters of God, beloved and lavished on by the Father.

2. **Form**—We have a human body, however through our spirit we can clothe ourselves with Christ and live out of His heavenly life and body.

3. **The Holy Spirit**—We are indwelt with the Spirit of God for life and ministry in the same way as Christ was, because He poured out the Spirit on His Church.

4. **Authority**—Christ has delegated His authority to us.

5. **Angels**—Angels serve and protect us and may, at times, facilitate the miraculous in and around us.

6. **The Scripts**—Christ has powerfully positioned us, so we get to play the part of the Hero as He did, so the power of the script can be manifests in us as favour and blessing.

7. **The Person of Christ**—Through unity and connection with His father in heaven, His words and actions may augment ours at times, to release wisdom and power on a whole other level.

So our potential is to "walk as Jesus walked," as John the Apostle invites us to do in his first letter.

Christ is our example, rather than an unattainable ideal—for us this is a life-changing shift in theological emphasis and perspective, but it is merely a beginning as we consider the full breadth of what God intends for us!

John 5, 8 & 14 | Eph 1-2 | Rom 13:14 | Gal 3:27 | 1 Cor 3:16 | Heb 1:14 | Gal 2:20
Phil 2:13 | | John 15:1-5 | 1 John 2:6

It is the life of the risen and glorified Son of God intertwined in and around our lives—His life shatters the ceiling of our expectations for what we can become in Him.

Sometimes in marriage the lines blur, to the point where whose thoughts and actions are whose, can be difficult to distinguish. The love and oneness and our pursuit of intimacy can diminish our sense of individual identity. It is good though, because in the middle of the mix we learn that two are better than one.

The same is true for us as we push into Christ. Every encounter brings us into conformity with the Son until even distinctions between His divine life and person and our own mortality and humanity become a tangled knot unable to be unravelled.

We are in training to become life-giving spirits, swept into heroism and blessed to the point of overwhelm—perfectly positioned for worshipful response.

Something wonderful happens—a miracle, or a breakthrough—and there are just so many incredible elements in play, we cannot be sure who or what deserves the credit.

Yet no matter how we look at it, and no matter how much we attain of it, there is a common theme.

It all comes back to the Hero.

Every good thing can be traced back somehow to one of His heroic decisions or acts. In the end, no matter how much He makes of us, He must receive all the credit—all the glory!

Rom 8:29 | 1 Cor 15:45-49

Q1.   In the week just passed, identify one of these elements at play in your circumstances?

Q2.   Which of these perspectives do you find the most difficult to accept, be thankful for, and use?

Q3.   Which do you value most and feel most inclined to seek?

Prayer.

Lord. It is the audacious cry of our heart—Christ, would You manifest yourself in us? Would You call angels to attend us, and would You grace us so we are more sensitive to the guidance of the Holy Spirit. We would walk in the authority and identity You have given, ever more comfortable with a life in line with Your own. Write Your law on our hearts and make us to be innately and intrinsically an object of Your good pleasure. It is our dearest wish to delight You and find joy in all You would have us walk in.   *Amen*

CHAPTER FIFTY-TWO

STEPPING FORWARD

OUR SPIRITUAL SENSES USE THE SAME INK
AND LAY A RECORD ALONGSIDE THOSE
ETCHED BY OUR PHYSICAL EXISTENCE.

When I worked for the Australian government, our family lived in Canberra. Life there was easy and relatively care-free. We reconnected with the Lord and pushed deeper into Him, and we enjoyed our young family as it grew, more than ever before.

I walked to and from work each day, taking a fairly direct line between the two points—along the shoulder of a freeway, over some very pleasant parkland, before I passed close to the lake and into the CBD.

In previous chapters I have connected the act as we enter into the heavenlies with the phenomenon of Christ inhabiting our life as His spirit dwells in us.

On my way home one day, I had my first real experience of the former. In our family, we have come to call the experience "going to Zion."

It began this way . . .

My mind had been troubled all afternoon with a sense of desire for God. My awareness of all the constraints my humanity put on our relationship was peaked.

I started home and pondered my desire to go deeper. The farther I walked the more frustrated I became with myself.

My steps took me through the parklands near Parliament House and past the residence of the Prime Minister. I descended the gravel verge and onto the asphalt of the freeway . . . the rhythm of my footsteps hypnotic.

I found myself mumbling . . .

"I feel so far away from You."

Over and over, the words left my lips, a strange mix of desire for God and dissatisfaction at the distance I lived from Him.

"Your world is so far from mine."

"It is like an unbridgeable chasm lies between us."

It startled me to see the chasm, but even so, I was not thrown out of my reverie.

I saw it before me, deep dark stone walls, they rose toward me from what seemed like bottomless depths. It was a misty and mystical atmosphere, and somehow dark and nearly sinister.

Beyond my awareness, my feet continued to journey home. Even the cars as they passed me at high speed could not disturb the moment!

Then I saw differently . . . not with physical eyes. I was in the spirit, and as such I experienced clarity without the detail we associate with our tangible senses. The closest thing I can compare it to is memory recall.

If yesterday we met a friend and had lunch, today we can still perceive the event as a memory. We could recall what happened, and even describe it in detail. In fact, memory is so convincing as a type of vision, we know it to be true even though the tangible evidence is no longer in front of us. We could and would swear to it in court if asked to do so.

Memory is the record of our story. Our five senses write words on its pages, and we are able to flick back through the pages nearly at will. In the spirit, our senses belonging to that realm use that same pen and ink—they lay a record of our story right alongside those etched by our physical existence. Whether we walk in the body or in the spirit, our memory faithfully captures the record of our every action. When we walk in the body our physical senses overwhelm our awareness of memory, but in the spirit we only have memory in real-time to guide us as to what happens. We write and read the story of our life simultaneously!

Back to the story of my first trip to Zion, and the dark stone walls of the chasm— and the mist . . .

"Your world is so far from mine."

"It is like an unbridgeable chasm lies between us."

But it wasn't unbridgeable. There was a bridge! It was made of rope and wooden boards and it stretched out, only to disappear into the mist.

"Your world is so far from mine."

"I want to get to You . . ."

I started across the bridge, stepping but getting nowhere.

"I'm stepping towards Your world."

Stepping, stepping . . .

Stepping . . .

"Your world is so far from mine."

"I want to get to You . . ."

Determination and desire. More steps.

Then I saw the other side, far away.

Hope and exaltation!

Stepping, stepping . . .

Stepping . . .

"Your world is so far from mine."

"I want to get to You . . ."

And then I arrived and stepped off the wooden boards onto a gravelly path. I was in another realm. The unseen realm. The bridge met a path where it branched away along the edge of the cliff in either direction. I decided to turn right and as I walked I noticed a bank slightly on my left, thickly forested. On the other side the chasm fell away. The path cut inland and upward away from the chasm and the bridge, and through the wood.

Then abruptly, the trees fell away and I burst into lush meadows, rolling away in every direction. Far in the distance mountains towered into the sky. Just down and to my right lay a truly wonderful city, walled and ancient in aspect but luminous and perfect in every way. I ran towards it, eager to explore its secrets . . .

Suddenly I realised I had arrived back home and the vision receded, but I had broken through! If it could happen once, I was determined, it could and would happen again!

Q1.   What do you know of Zion?

Q2.   Does God and His heavenly abode feel near or far to you?

Q3.   What is your story of entering in?

Prayer.

Lord. We want to make Your world our own, to be natives of the realms You inhabit. Make us fearless in our pursuit of heaven. Fix our eyes and minds on what is above and catch us up so we can walk with You in white, as the spirits of just men and women made perfect, in You Christ Jesus.   Amen.

CHAPTER FIFTY-THREE

LIVING ON THE EDGE

IT WAS A REAL CHALLENGE TO
CONCENTRATE ON WORK WITH
THIS DECISION LOOMING OVER ME.

We were expecting Liberty, our youngest child and after being in Canberra away from grandparents for a little over three years we decided to return home and move back to Brisbane where our families lived. Wouldn't it be great to have this baby surrounded by family . . ?

I needed a new job—a more difficult ask in Brisbane than in the country's capital.

I put out some feelers, and then, through a sweet confluence of events I was offered a job in a technology consultancy. This was a multi-national company, so yes, we could live in Brisbane, but I would have to travel to where the work was. For up to twelve weeks at a time, I would leave early on a Monday morning and arrive back home late on a Thursday night.

Great! We could move home.

But travelling so much for work? Hmmm. I was uncomfortable with the thought. It didn't sit well with me. Even though I had never really thought about it, I realised I had a conviction in my mind that good Christian men don't travel for work. Good fathers and husbands were present for their families. Besides, I didn't trust myself to be away so often and for so long at a stretch. Who would voluntarily put themselves in a position where they would be subject to all the temptations associated with men who travel for work?

It was a private conversation in my head, not exactly a mature and well thought through point of view, but it was there.

It resolved into a simple thought. To choose this was to live on the edge.

But why welcome risk into your family and personal life? Why would you chose to live on the edge?

I had no answer so I hesitated, unable to proceed.

My potential employer waited to hear back from me.

Anya was excited. From her perspective it was all coming together.

Meanwhile, I was trying to get things done, trying to concentrate on my job with this whole decision looming—still walking to work each day.

This particular day, I felt the pull of heaven on my way there and diverted to the park, crossing it until I got to the lake edge.

I stood there looking over the water, searching for peace or whatever it was I needed to make a decision, and in that moment, heaven and earth met once again.

It was as though the lakeside pathway I stood on became the edge of the chasm I had so recently encountered. The bridge was there before me. I answered the invitation and this time I crossed it easily.

In the spirit, I paused at the other side. Which way should I go?

Last time I had turned to the right. This time, I turned left.

The edge of the chasm was level, but it meandered from side to side.

The path followed it. Where did this lead? Was Zion actually a proper land, a realm, rather than just the city I had seen the other day?

I turned a corner and was shocked at what I saw.

A figure sat on a picnic rug on a patch of grass between the path and the chasm. There was a basket on the rug, food and drink all unpacked and spread out.

Jesus and a picnic. His face held a grin—so unexpected!

He beckoned me closer and I sat as my mind struggled to keep up. Then He spoke . . .

"I am with you, on the edge."

Then everything freeze-framed, and He and the wonderful place suddenly all just vanished and I was back beside the lake.

I reflected on what I had experienced. We had sat on the edge of the chasm— the edge. And He had said, "I am with you on the edge."

I hadn't wanted to travel for work, to live so close to the edge. *Hmmph*. Smart, and a little funny!

But, okay then.

I had heard enough.

I hurried off to work and called the consultancy during my lunch hour . . .

      . . . to tell them I would take their job.

Q1.   What fear you face today could be answered by the resources and perspectives from heaven?

Q2.   In what ways do physical limitations and circumstances influence your decision-making process?

Q3.   Have you ever had an intimate spiritual encounter? What changed for you afterwards and why?

Prayer.

Lord. We repent of small minded and earthy reason. Transform our minds and set them on pure and holy thoughts. Snatch us up from the squeeze and conformity of worldly logic and teach us of Your higher ways. We desire to embrace the foolishness of God which is wiser than human wisdom and philosophy, and to become graduates of the School of Christ, and those who know the deep truths of Your kingdom.   Amen.

CHAPTER FIFTY-FOUR

THE SETUP

HE WAS THE ANOINTING. HIS TOUCH CAUSED THE HEROES OF OLD TO RISE IN FAITH AND GREATNESS.

We take a deep breath, our heart beating in time with heaven, awash with possibility and promise, our mind tuned to that dimension. Yes, we chose to live beyond ourselves—to walk as Jesus walked. Our quiet but sure, "Yes", rings out, and we surrender to the One who reaches to take control, and in so doing consecends to put on flesh again.

And so the dance begins. We're taking our place in Christ in the heavenlies—rooted and grounded there, entirely free at last. The grasp of cause and curse and consequences fall away as we are rooted and grounded in love, lavishly blessed before the Father. We are enriched—body, soul and spirit—as our life becomes intertwined with that of the Hero. As we practically relinquish control of what we used to hold so tightly, allowing Him to take the reigns and glorify Himself in our lives, our emptiness is filled with heaven's overflow—love that surpasses knowledge, joy unspeakable, and peace that passes understanding. Our circumstances no longer shape our destiny or situation!

We have been set up for success . . .

A lot has gone into positioning us in this way, but ultimately we find ourselves here because two others have taken up their very specific positions—the Holy Spirit needed to come to earth and into our innermost being, and Christ had to rise and ascend and take His place on heaven's throne.

They were there at creation, working together; even still they unite to weave beauty out of what is often dark and empty.

Eph 3:19 | 1 Peter 1:8 | Phil 4:7 | Hebrews 8:1 | Hebrews 12:2

The Spirit was there rejoicing alongside the Hero, informing the design of the work of His hands, as the architect at His side. Humility as a force to undergird the mechanics of creation was His idea. It was He who suggested the Hero and the Father's story should flavour everything we see around us in the world.

He was the anointing. His touch caused the heroes of old to rise in faith and greatness, one at a time. I see Him at work in the ministry of Jesus, connecting Christ to heaven and serving as an adviser by His side.

Who better to pour out the Spirit on the heads of all of us, than He who valued His influence above all others? The Hero!

> The Holy Spirit had to come!

Now, as the personification of wisdom, the Holy Spirit is in us. He leads us into all truth. The Hero is the ultimate subject of the scripts, but the Holy Spirit designed them and owns them. He knows their every nuance. No one can master them without His guidance. Without Him, any sense of the scripts leads to law-keeping or superstition. At best this leaves the devotee in a posture expectant of recompense, a stance not born of humility. Counterintuitively, they find themselves on the villain script and their tireless efforts curse instead of saving their futures.

Those who are filled with the Spirit, on the other hand, find themselves under the influence of one whose passionate trust and adoration of the Father is contagious. His perfect knowledge of the stories and scripts is written on our hearts. It drives us to our knees and then onto our faces. Desperate for God, we find ourselves worshippers—we begin to seek holiness and wholeness for their own sake. We open ourselves up for the Holy Spirit to cleanse us of our brokenness, our wounds and our shame. He is delighted to respond. He heals and frees us . . . beyond our expectations.

The Hero is the Good Shepherd who starts us on our journey, seeking us out as lost sheep and bringing us into the fold.

Then the Holy Spirit takes over . . .

Like the woman who cleans house, He sanctifies us and prepares us to walk in the spirit—to enter into the Father's house. Yet, what He *does* excites me less than what He *doesn't* do.

Prov 8:14-21 | Jer 31:33-34 | John 16:13 | Gal 3:10 | Luke 15

He doesn't clean house for the fun of it. The Holy Spirit is not a clean freak! He does not clean me up because He detests all my mess—He has a more wonderful purpose. He cleans away the dust and grime, and the moment He finds the treasure of who I am, the real me, He stops His work and starts to dance around in joy. The dirt is forgotten. He is too busy dialling up the angels to invite them over for a party to even think of putting away the mop and broom!

Another one is ready to stand before the Father!

The Holy Spirit leads us into all truth—truth about who we have become, and who we are as we are transformed and aligned to God's intention. He teaches us who we are in Christ, and prepares our hearts and minds for the journey heavenward. He brings heaven into our spirits and releases us to soar! He finds us confused, remakes us, and leaves us all wrapped up in Christ so that our lives are intertwined.

The Holy Spirit needed to come, but for everything to work as intended, Christ needed to be positioned too.

He needed to go!

And so, he rose, ascended, and sat upon the throne of heaven, taking his place to rule and reign as a king, but also as priest sitting there to mediate a covenant through his ongoing intercession—as we dispossess him in multiple ways.

That priestly intercession combines the idea of intertwined lives as we are united into Christ's body, as well as Him having an ongoing role presenting His sacrifice so that we can be accepted as blameless before the Father. Our priestly mediator stands between earth and heaven to mediate both our standing and our passage into the heavenlies.

Christ remains as human. Why? Because in concert with the Holy Spirit, Christ's unity of form with us allows a community rather than one invidual at a time to connect to heaven. He needed to go, and there He stays. Christ has cancelled all His travel plans, so that heaven can be ours today and every day of our lives.

Together, they share a wonderful common purpose. As they assume their positions on the field, they inspire us to do the same, to take advantage of all they have laboured long to achieve. And so, we reach out to lay hold of that for which Christ Jesus laid hold of us.

Luke 15:8-10 | Hebrew 7:25 | Phil 3:12

Q1.   Is the Holy Spirit your friend and companion, or do you keep Him at arm's length?

Q2.   What is the greatest influence or experience that has shaped your relationship with the Holy Spirit?

Q3.   What is your response to heaven's endeavours to give you standing there? How are you positioning yourself and leaning into the invitation?

Prayer.

Lord. We welcome the Holy Spirit into our life. Fill us afresh. Cleanse, purify and remove everything set to hide the treasure of who we were made to be. Comfort and guide us and fit us to stand before the Father. We honour You as the Spirit of wisdom and the Architect of all the cause and effect able to shapes our lives. Teach us to walk in line with Your preferences and prepare us for all of our life and walk and calling. Stay close and show us the way we should go, every day, every hour of our lives.   Amen.

CHAPTER FIFTY-FIVE

DOUBLE TAKE

THERE IS NOW NO LIMIT TO THE REACH
OF THE HERO, AND THAT LEAVES US WITH
A NEW VISION AND CATCH CRY.

Remember the story of Ezekiel, and the very familiar valley of dry bones? We love that chapter—nothing is impossible if we will only believe! So true, yet it is the darndest thing for us to plot a course between the disappointments and the breakthrough victory we seek.

Sometimes we are required to wait on a miracle; other times necessitate our rising in faith and acting in obedience to usher one in. Truth be told, sometimes we end up daunted and a bit paralysed because the dry bones of our circumstances seem a little far gone.

We have plenty of good days, glorious times where we feel so blessed and are so thankful. But things aren't always the way they are meant to be. Some stuations, like a poorly-trained hound, get entirely out of hand and wreak havoc. At those times, caught amongst our questions, and feeling the tension between the many facets of understanding of the character of God, we try to make sense of life.

Ezekiel is looking down, perilously balancing on a rare patch of grass between the remains of two fallen warriors, bones bleached by the sun. Rippling out so far in every direction, filling the valley, in fact, are so many more—death and defeat surround him on every side.

The Lord startles him with a redemptive question that explores the extent of his expectation:

"Can these bones live?"

Ezek 37:1-14

And so, we locate the apparent moral of this story, that God has higher expectations in our situations than we do. So, it follows that we should, hope, dream, and rise in faith!

These bones, of course, can stand for anything that has gone haywire. Yes, we believe that the Almighty can unscramble the eggs. We might go further and affirm that if we can only go spiritual, we can circumvent the impossible. I, for one, love that perspective. We might break out in worship to move a mountain, or speak a word of faith to shape an alternative future. All of that seems appropriate to me, yet I sense there is something greater at play here.

Those bones are not primarily speaking hope into a trying relationship, a prodigal child, an incurable disease, a marriage on the rocks, or a train wreck of a career. Sure, it works, and we can apply this chapter in those ways, but this is not a valley filled with those things. It is a valley full of people—a multitude of warriors that are not fulfilling their purpose—dead people. There is no fight left in them. They cannot heed a call or draw their weapons. In fact, they are so far gone that everything about them has long atrophied and decayed. They are past feeling or knowing, and the dominion they were charged to protect is defenceless.

If these bones are to be restored, if all these fallen warriors can be raised, it will be a miracle of life and dominion anew! As all those lives stand together, they will not form a rabble crowd. They will stand armed and dangerous as an army in ranks, ready to contend passionately for crown and empire!

There is hope here, even though the world, the church, and our lives and families are more broken than we would like to admit. The Father's expectations are more incredible, more immeasurable, than we can ask or imagine.

Enter the Hero.

The world was a mess. The incarnation of Christ changed everything. He appeared, and took in hand an aspect of the backstory of God—dispossession— that others found unwieldy, mastering it to the point of using it to shape our standing and future. Ultimately it is through a twofold dispossession of His life that we are able to enter into all Christ has for us.

Then, in our intimacy with the Father and also in our intercession before Him we also dispossess the villain twofold as well.

The law of sin and death, and the law of the spirit of life, contend with

Eph 3:20-21

one another for our future. One law authorises us to fight and subvert the other which would leave us cursed, condemned, ruined and destroyed. The villain brought us under threat. The Hero delivers us into freedom and victory.

We reach for Christ's life in the heavenlies and He takes hold of ours.

Through the adequacy of the Hero, the Father is surrounded by family, a community snatched from the hands of the enemy. Each feast testifies to the ongoing triumph of the Son—the number of heavenly guests swells toward its original measure. We too are part of His triumph. We have finally been brought near, as His beloved sons and daughters. Curse and consequence continue to lose their hold as we enjoy a lifestyle of rising into His presence where we are loved indescribably, our lives intertwined with His. We live out of the rich joy that is His life above.

We have life, and we have it abundantly!

He lives out his desires through our mouths and bodies, and in this way heroism takes root in us. We rise out of defeat and hopelessness as a mighty army of powerful warriors, each and every one possessing within their being the person and potential of the glorious Son.

What a masterful and powerful plan, one that causes us to gasp in delight, that births hope into every circumstance within our lives, our families and indeed, our world.

Then we suddenly do a double take . . .

We realise that all of this comes to us as a invitation whispered quietly by one who has stooped low, holding our destiny gently within His outstretched hand, leaving us overwhelmed in worship.

As we respond with humble affirmation, there is now no limit to the reach of the Hero. At last we stand upon our feet—a vast army, with a new vision and catch cry:

"Heroes All"!

John 10:10

Q1.   What impacted you most as you read this book?

Q2.   What is the best way you can put that truth into practice in you life? What do you intend to do, and when will you begin?

Q3.   What is it about the Hero that captures your imagination the most? How could you best respond to that?

Prayer.

Lord. We are thankful to have beheld Your heart. Thank You for sharing your backstory with us. We feel privileged and humbled. We rise up in worship to glorify the Hero. It is our furvent prayer that He would be formed in us. Grace us for all that needs to take place in us for that to be the case. Christ, we embrace You and Your life and all that You are. Help us to lose ourselves there and step into the full measure of Your desires for us.   Amen.

HERO WORSHIP

The four living creatures, each having six wings, were full of eyes around and within. And they do not rest day or night, saying:

"Holy, holy, holy,

Lord God Almighty,

Who was and is and is to come!"

Whenever the living creatures give glory and honor and thanks to Him who sits on the throne, who lives forever and ever, the twenty-four elders fall down before Him who sits on the throne and worship Him who lives forever and ever, and cast their crowns before the throne, saying:

"You are worthy, O Lord,

To receive glory and honor and power;

For You created all things,

And by Your will they exist and were created."

Revelation 4:8-11

I bind to myself today . . . The virtue of the Incarnation of Christ with His Baptism, The virtue of His crucifixion with His burial, The virtue of His Resurrection with His Ascension, The virtue of His coming on the Judgement Day . . . I invoke today all these virtues, Against every hostile merciless power Which may assail my body and my soul . . . Against every knowledge that binds the soul of man.

Christ, protect me today . . . That I may receive abundant reward.

Christ with me, Christ before me,

Christ behind me, Christ within me,

Christ beneath me, Christ above me,

Christ at my right, Christ at my left . . .

Christ in the heart of everyone who thinks of me,

Christ in the mouth of everyone who speaks to me,

Christ in every eye that sees me,

Christ in every ear that hears me . . .

From St Patrick's Breastplate (Prayer from the 5th Century)

NOTE FROM THE AUTHOR

While I find the reflections of this book orientating, they also overwhelm me. For me it is a whispered invitation into more, one that I endeavour each day to respond to with all the humility and furvour I can muster. For me, this is a rich vein of truth that will take a lifetime to unearth. It is my prayer that, just as you have journeyed with me through these pages, you would also travel alongside so that as a growing community we can quest together for all that is true for us in Christ.

The Laodocean temptation to resist the compulsion of Christ's desire to take hold of our life is one I too struggle with. I am thankful that I now understand what it is and what it could be. I hope you will join me as I try to master the art of laying down my life so I can find it afresh.

I find much here that encourages me that I can punch above my weight and contribute something in this generation that is preserved into those that will follow after.

Whatever there is that you feel you can take away from these pages, my hope and prayer is that you are blessed by it and find yourself flying a little nearer to the flame as a result. May it bring you into more joy, more peace, more hope, greater usefulness, and most of all, may the Hero fill your vision so that your worship is enriched . . .

JEFFREY MCKEE

Jeffrey McKee writes with fresh insight into the biblical narrative. His heart is to equip and inspire others toward maturity in their faith. He and his wife, Anya are the founders of TORN CURTAIN COLLECTIVE, a ministry that equips and inspires God's people to live as confidently in the spiritual realm as they do in the physical. Their passion is to help people discover healing and freedom and find their comfort zone on the cutting edge. They live with their four children in Wellington, New Zealand.

www.torncurtain.co.nz

Lightning Source UK Ltd.
Milton Keynes UK
UKHW011858161220
375343UK00001B/15